People, Not Psychiatry

People
Not
Psychiatry

Michael Barnett

WITHDRAWN

London   George Allen & Unwin Ltd
Ruskin House   Museum Street

ISBN 0 04 616013 2 Hardback
     0 04 616014 0 Paperback

Printed in Great Britain
in 11 point Baskerville type by
Clarke, Doble & Brendon Ltd
Plymouth

Preface

All writing is about oneself. Our experiences are always there, between paper and pen. And yet we all, more or less, confuse our perspective with truth or reality, and try to get that perspective confirmed as true or real by others. Like Freud, we can all explain everyone else away with our own view of the world.

So we have schizophrenic psychiatrists calling schizophrenics prophets and seers; and psychiatrists obsessed with power, status and prestige magnifying their own mystique and the helplessness of patients. I read a book of essays on schizophrenia, and each essay is a small autobiography, a miniature confession.

In view of the ineluctability of the subject, this book eschews the objective. Its perspectives are highly personal, and so is much of the material. I make no apology for this unless it proves to be boring.

Much of this book is a living story, concerning living people. To avoid offence and distress many names have been changed. To those friends and others who appear here without disguise I would like to both affirm and apologize for a partiality of my perspective. I hope I have not been unjust.

I want to thank my friends Joanna Clelland and David Eddy for the time, skill and energy they gave me in reading the manuscript and offering many useful criticisms. Also my thanks to Juliet Forman for her generous help with the proofs.

Finally, here, I would like to thank Peter Leek of George Allen and Unwin, for his patience and faith.

To Sam and Fli and all in
PNP – with apologies.

Also to the late Fritz Perls,
Dionysian, who gave me,
through his books, the
courage to write what I felt,
and to Jean-Paul Sartre,
Apollonian, who,
unbeknown to him, kept me
within limits.

Contents

*To be sure health is the only
allowable ideal, the only one
to which what I call man
has a right to aspire, but
when it is given in a human
being from the very
beginning, it hides half the
world from him*

Jacques Rivière
in a letter to Antonin Artaud

Introduction

This book is about people and psychiatry.

Psychiatry is one of that nest of subsystems we call society. Actually *society* does not exist. It is just a metaphor for you and me acting in certain (patterned) ways, or socially. Likewise psychiatry, as a concrete reality, does not exist. It is simply an elite group thinking and acting in patterns, with the rest of us colluding. In real terms psychiatry has the substantiality of a soap bubble.

Like its ugly sister, sociology, psychiatry aims at being scientific. In doing this, likewise it omits the person, the unique you, the unique me. Men create science, society, psychiatry; then these, like Frankensteins, turn and run the show. I am my shadow's shadow. Man puts his life and his power into his ideas, his abstract inventions, then slavishly obeys them, as if they are real. This is reification. Once it was the stars, sun, thunder; then mythic gods, sacred animals; today it is abstractions to which we give our life and our strength – and our blame. We abdicate our humanity. Who today dares to be fully human?

The process of diagnosis in psychiatry is to an extent political. Today's 'sick' are often the socially useless. Meanwhile power maniacs remain at large, frequently as social successes. Nevertheless the suffering and terrors of neuroses and psychoses are real enough, and not to be converted, as some have tried to convert them, into myths of a new *élitism*. As for treatment and prescription in psychiatry, these are almost always politically defined. Political psychiatry says : when *this* happens or is so, *this* is done. To act otherwise is to feel in opposition, the crushing weight of mass and power attitudes.

But people are beginning to leave home in unprecedented numbers. In this case 'home' is the *status quo*, the way things are done. People are walking out on all this and taking decisions for themselves based – which society certainly isn't – on their own experience.

Out of this migration, this emergence or rebirth from the agglutinous suck of society, have come some real alternatives in or to psychiatry, or rather, to the healing of the psyche. The entire Human Potential or Encounter Movement represents a totally new approach towards psycho-emotional disturbance and distress. From words and theory it moves to experience and praxis; from a general methodology to the individual person. It is the human revolution in action, just as clinical psychiatry is the counter-revolution in action, in whose methods and goals stultification, suppression, frustration, constriction and adaptation are all to be seen.

Another natural efflorescence of this tide moving away from the expert towards the person are the PNP networks – People, Not Psychiatry. The movement was initiated by the writer in July 1969, and since then some ten thousand people, I should say, have made contact with one or other of its networks. In the meantime more and more people descend on the Growth centres to try Encounter and its allied methods such as Bio-energetics and Gestalt – and many of them stay, changing radically and enriching the ways in which they experience themselves and the world.

In the light of all this, who can doubt that such alternatives are needed and desired?

The days of corrective psychiatry are numbered.

This book is about people and psychiatry. It is about the writer's experience of them both, separately and in concert. It contains part of the PNP story – how it began and grew and changed – *as the writer experienced it*. In it there are frequent references to Growth centres and the whole movement that is sheering away from the paternal – and for many people omnipotent – psychiatrist with his 'I know what's best for you' approach – just like the Mum and Dad we have to learn to leave.

To leave home, and become independently ourselves, is to leave the psychiatrist behind, along with Mum and Dad, the politician, and Auntie Flo. Each of us has to find his or her own centre, and live from that. We have to stand alone, maybe alongside others, yet still alone. Only then can we at last begin to move towards fulfilment, self-realization, our own original nature that we have lost and long to recover so desperately.

We are born separate and whole,[1] but *into* society. Our nature is shaped in patterned ways. We act blindly, mechanically, as we have been taught and told. We do not 'interact with our environment' from our centre but instead respond as expected and required for much of the time.

From this state of sleep a delivery is needed, a rebirth. Man, born into society, needs to be reborn out of society, if he is to become what he is. Then, fearless and whole, he can return and enrich the world. In the East they know about this : it is the Moslem mystic going into the desert, the Hindu into the mountains; it is the Bodhisattva of Mahayana Buddhism who devotes himself to his own Enlightenment and then reaching the threshold of *nirvana,* turns back in order to help all other sentient beings to attain it.

In the West we are far from this. We have been hurled fast and furious into feverish lives of activity until we no longer know who we are. The first step in finding out is to leave home. So let us do so. It is time.

[1] If man was not innately whole he would not have emerged out of nature.

Air

The first real contact I had with psychiatry was back in 1965, in Australia. I was in Sydney. I had come there after six months in Perth and short stays in Adelaide and Melbourne. My wife Pamela had been doing a series of meaningless jobs to keep us, whilst I wrote. I had been writing for about two years on and off, whilst travelling through the East prior to Perth, and I thought it was about time I did something for the exchequer. Also, we were desperate to get away from Australia, and we needed money for that. I got a job teaching mathematics at a girls' high school.

First morning I was there, right away whilst being briefed by the Head of Department on my classes, I was struck by a slicing pain in the gut and collapsed in a heap. I couldn't move. I struggled, as my mother had taught me, but I was completely paralysed by the pain. I was carried to the sick room and laid out on the bed. They drew the curtains and left me. Immediately I wanted to go to the can but couldn't move. My stomach wanted to get out through my rectum. It was pushing for total evacuation. Eventually I crawled, moaning, to the toilet and opened up. I thought I was dying. I would have been glad to. I crawled back to the bed and then the emptiness wanted to come out, so I had to get back to the can. This happened a few times. This great drama being played out that no one else knew about. I don't know where it all came from – military evacuations. And all the time the knife was hacking away in my guts, whilst the rest of me felt like stone. What a mess. Everything in me wanted to do something different : teach, lie still, shit, hack, moan, go home, be brave, cry. What was going on ? They called the doctor.

15

The minute he walked in I leapt to my feet, patted him on the back so that his stethoscope swung, smiled all round, said I was fine, and three minutes later was in a classroom teaching.

Later on after hours I went to see the doctor, to pay him, and he shelled me out some pills. He said I needed calming down, I was hyperactive. I took the pills for a few days but they made me feel woolly and numb and full of dry pith. I went back and told him. He said I should persevere. Then he said, 'Are you always like this?' I said, 'What d'you mean? What d'you mean? What d'you mean?' He looked at me appraisingly, probably considering whether to certify me or not, then he sighed, and turned away, and sorted out some more pills. 'Take these as well as the others,' he said. Later I flushed the lot away.

But I got into some pretty weird states in Sydney. For instance I used to climb up on top of the wardrobe and sit there meditating, crosslegged, with wild eyes and my mind afire. There seemed nothing strange in this to me. It was very quiet and calm up there, and I could see everything. Also I used to have what I took to be mystical experiences. I would feel charged like a meteor, or a shooting star, in contact with the source of life energy. I was writing some extraordinary things at this time, stories made up about people that seemed to be living in my mind and had just got a chance to talk and tell of themselves. I used to climb down off the wardrobe, sit at the typewriter, and my fingers would type all these odd stories and pieces out. Soon something cohesive started to emerge and ended up as the first draft of a crazy unpublished novel. Seven years later I can still bear it, it still makes me laugh – and as a rule I cannot bear what I have written yesterday, let alone last week or last month.

Then there was the time I collapsed in the middle of the night on the bathroom floor. I couldn't move. I could talk but my whole body seemed paralysed. Pam tried hard not to freak, but eventually called the hospital. I had been lying there a long time, though quite calm, and able to talk to her. I looked up to find two uniformed attendants and a stretcher. I bawled at them to go away. They pushed and edged their way into the bathroom, which was small, but I yelled at them I couldn't be moved. They tried to persuade me, saying it would be easy to slide me on to the stretcher, but I said I refused to be moved an inch. I told them to go away, 'Go away!' gushing out of my paralysed body like fire from a dragon at bay. They looked at Pam, shrugged, half amused, and went out, left.

Ten minutes later I was up and dancing, flapping around free as a bird.

Also I had this very odd relationship with our cat, Gandhi. Pam had brought her home one night, a grocer's stray. Before long I was communicating with that cat as if we were superimposed. Somehow we met in the middle, between cat and human, and there we fought out our complex relationship of hate and love, of independence and power. I have always been a cat man, though less so now. A year and a half earlier in Assam there had been my aunt's cat, Topsy, one of a half dozen, who had slept with me every night for two months until Pam arrived out from England, whereupon Topsy took off, ran away. She came back later but refused to look me in the eye until I left. But with Gandhi it was very highpowered. I was caught up in my relationsbip with her in a way that made me feel out of control. I suppose Sydney was the peak of my schizoid phase, the nearest I got to schizophrenia. It was also a very exciting period, with things happening and experiences felt and images that I haven't grasped even yet. It was painful, beautiful, rich, arid, terrifying, powerful. But I went through it. No one stepped in and stopped me, which is what usually happens. No one cut me off from my natural movement and pointed me back, or in the direction *they* thought I should take, which is what usually happens. I was lucky. Every time I experience someone else being thwarted in this, stymied, blocked, sent back by the raised hand, the drug, the white coat, turned away from the freeway and being told it is a cul-de-sac, or that entry is *verboten*, I want to rant and weep.

I do not believe objectivity is ever possible, though many books aim for it, and some even pretend they have achieved it. Personally, I am not even going to aim for it. This book is about me. It is about me and my experience of certain events and people, and in talking about these, I am talking about me. Just as in the way you respond to what I say you are talking about you.

Since perspective is always latent I might as well make mine manifest. So I am going to say to begin with a few things about myself, how I feel about psychiatry, mental illness, the world in general, and myself. After that will come my propaganda, personal and ideological. Watch out for me. I can be a fast convincing talker. *Caveat lector*. Beware reader.

Good, now you trust me, since you see how open I am. So now you really have to watch out.

I believe that there are such things as neuroses, and I describe or define neuroses as organic subsystems that impair or impede full growth, that is, the full free functioning of the total, or central, organic life system. We are born with life, and life wants to go on. Life is energy, and energy by its nature will, without obstruction, run its course.

Unfortunately this energy meets other energy which is, or is seen as, threatening. So the organism takes evasive action. It shuts itself up or off, it locks itself away, preserves what it has got, stops growing for fear it may be destroyed. It can even shrink itself in the hope that this way it will not be seen, and thereby escape. Or it camouflages itself as a good citizen, a likeable fellow, an obedient slave. Out of these actions come artificial subsystems that stand for ourselves.

These strangling and constricting subsystems are us too. We put them there. They were not imposed upon us from outside, though we may pretend they were, and though we may have built them *in response to* the outside. Since they are us then, we have to accept responsibility for them, and since they are us we can, presumably, remove them any time. This notion of taking full responsibility for everything we are now is at the root of the Gestalt method of therapy. You can read all about it in the works of Fritz Perls.

Gestalt therapy, focusing as it does simply on the here and

18

now, does not admit the significance of traumas in our lives. Here is Fritz Perls on them :

'The great error of psychoanalysis is in assuming that the memory is reality. All the so-called *traumata*, which are supposed to be the root of the neurosis, are an invention of the patient to save his self-esteem. None of these traumata has ever been proved to exist. I haven't seen a single case of infantile trauma that wasn't a falsification. They are all lies to be hung on to in order to justify one's unwillingness to grow. To mature means to take responsibility for your life, to be on your own. Psychoanalysis fosters the infantile state by considering that the past is responsible for the illness.'[1]

I do not entirely agree with Perls. But the position he takes has in the past been very much neglected in favour of others that emphasize the helplessness and impotence of the patient in contrast to the status and omnipotence of the therapist or analyst. You need an expert to help you uncover and understand your past, we were told. Then, after hundreds of pounds, if not years, you know yourself, and knowing, change, or accept that you can't.[2] Gestalt cuts through all this heavy dependency and weary dissection and says : this is how you are; this is what you are doing; it is destructive and delusional, disordered and phoney, antilife; what are you going to do about changing it, if it is change you want?

In practice it is not so easy. Powerful forces keep us in the ruts of our habitual patterns. Many of these patterns we set up in response to early experiences, which can be called traumas. Knowing about them, through insight therapy, doesn't help much, is only a beginning. But living through them again, and *seeing* (experiencing) that the earlier actions taken in the face of them *are not necessary for survival*, can lead to the weakening of the stunting subsystems, and perhaps their eventual dispersal. This view is central to Primal therapy[3] and to the Bioenergetic approach.[4]

[1] *Gestalt Therapy Verbatim.*
[2] Usually little or nothing changes because, for the organism as a totality, *little or nothing has changed*.
[3] Created by Arthur Janov. See Bibliography.   [4] See below.

It is my belief that behind every neurosis lies fear. Our subsystems are meant to preserve us. We block because we fear to be what we are : angry, loving, grieving, hating, joyful, despairing, egotistical, laughing, fearing, marvelling human beings. We even fear to fear. And we fear to experience the intense joy and the intense pain of human living.

Every time we block through fear we set up a new neurotic subsystem or reinforce an existing one. The healthy response to threat, danger, is fight or flight. Action. When we freeze, ignore, hide, panic, distort, defend at arm's length, this is anti-life.

The logic at work in infancy is the creature of need and dependency. Dependency lives under a shadow of calamity. If I need you I am perpetually expecting the worst to happen. My life becomes devoted to keeping you sweet, or at least *there*. If I truly believe I need you to survive, I will do *anything* to preserve your presence. Even effectively annihilate my essence. Existence before essence, as the neurotic existentialists say. Existence is consciousness, essence only life. Without the first, I fear I shall die. Without the second, I may be a simulacrum, but I am alive.

In infancy there is prolonged dependency, vulnerability, unremitting fear of the calamitous action. Steps are taken to avoid the worst, patterns set up that pre-empt the future. The child is father to the man.

Later, the man has to father both man and child.

In the meantime, a therapist might be used.

The cure to neurosis lies in dispersing or breaking the destroying systems, leaving the life-loving forces free to spread and grow.[5]

Many methods help to do this – a little. The task is enormous, and takes total devotion. Nothing short of a life commitment can succeed, in my opinion. Perhaps that is part of what

---

[5] A whole complex of patterns supports the child-built structure of being. There is inter-maintenance, so modification is difficult. Possibly, if we can contact the deeper, purer energy that expresses itself in an original unadulterated fashion, and live by it, we can, to an extent, dodge the patterned column.

we are here for. The Hindus and Buddhists look at it differently and call it *karma*.

Drugs at best *appear* to achieve results. But since they are not concerned with the experiences that produced the state of being, the experiences that live in every cell and every fibre, nor concerned with *experientially* changing that state, they can achieve nothing of any deep or lasting value.

Rats under stress (tied to a board) were given tranquillizers. The apparent result : they seemed indifferent to their situation. The underlying reality : stress hormones were still being produced at a high rate. Manifest behaviour can be a poor guide to phenomenological reality.

Mechanistic methods like drugs and electro-treatment treat man as a machine. But I am not a machine, and neither are you, whether you agree to being treated like one or not.

Psychoanalysis and psychotherapy of the conventional kind can help, but not much. It is not only the emphasis they place on verbalization and cognitive understanding that limits these methods, it is also the ultimate poverty and unreality of the relationship between patient and analyst or therapist that prevents them from achieving valuable results rapidly. I consider the relationship between client and conventional therapist to be impoverished and unreal because we do not have here two persons meeting, opening, experiencing, flowing, interacting, but one person and one phantasmagoria, or phantom, who by being absent keeps control. How can a patient experience his interpersonal reality when the immediate interpersonal environment is so artificial? At some point, if not always, the therapist must himself become real if the patient's experience with him is to touch him and change him as a total person. The therapist's best weapon is his own reality, his own total presence made manifest to the patient. Anger, fear, hope, love, exasperation, delight – all these, and everything – the therapist should show when he feels them so that in that intense therapeutic situation the patient is forced to confront what he is spending his life running away from and avoiding – reality. His own and the world's.

This is Impact therapy, which I freely use. Other methods

I trust to bring to awareness, and change, petrified patterns both manifest and latent, both behavioural and phenomenological, are Encounter, Bioenergetics, Gestalt therapy, Primal therapy, Symboldrama, Psychodrama, Psychofantasy. And any settings that offer opportunity to take risks, to experiment with new and richer patterns, or with confusion, or with surrender of control and trust in the workings of reality, of what *is*, alongside others experimenting likewise, are allies of these experiential methods of therapy. The PNP network, or People Not Psychiatry, was an attempt to provide such settings together with reciprocal confirmation and concern.

'The basis of man's life with man is twofold, and it is one – the wish of every man to be confirmed as what he is, even as what he can become, by men; and the innate capacity in man to confirm his fellow-men in this way. That this capacity lies so immeasurably fallow constitutes the real weakness and questionableness of the human race; actual humanity exists only where this capacity unfolds.'[6]

To return to what we left behind, to our original nature, takes work of a monumental kind. In Growth centres, in PNP, people pool their energy. This energy can be tapped by all to make breakthroughs they could not make on their own. What we have here is a society of energy.

I want to refer briefly to two other radical views of mental illness. Szasz, the American psychiatrist,[7] sees mental sickness as a choice of being in the world. That is, people may choose deliberately to be mentally ill because of the rewards that social role brings them in diminished responsibility, in being cared for and given attention, or they have chosen the role because they have not learnt well enough the game of life and so have to settle for the subordinate status of the inadequate. Such a status is granted to the mentally ill, so some elect to play that game. As for psychiatry, this, according to Szasz, is a pseudo-medical enterprise pursued by certain persons for self-seeking

[6] Martin Buber, *The Knowledge of Man*.
[7] For some of his written works, see Bibliography.

interests of status and power. Those who pretend to be mentally ill, who present their calls for help, that is, in regulation
ways, need not psychiatry but an education, lessons in living
and in learning how to take control of their own lives.

Laing, who has contributed so much to turning psychiatry
turtle, churning the whole field up so that it was forced to find
new directions, uses several approaches that overlap and inter-
twine. One of these, which could be called the antipodean, or
even the absolution, approach, gives madness, especially in
schizophrenic dress, a super-status. Schizophrenia becomes the
negation of the negation, the rejection of alienation, the
struggle for sanity and reality. Laing attempts to do for the
schizophrenic much the same as Colin Wilson tried to do for
the outsider seventeen years ago[8] – give him grandeur and glory
and a 'one-of-the-chosen' tag.

The trouble with both these approaches is that they seem
to disregard or dodge the actual plight of the neurotic. He is
in pain, and he is missing out. True, he is also raking in, as I
discovered in Sydney. But what is a personal plot to the human
park? The edge of the garden need not be lined with stones.
Shared reality is not to be too readily forsaken. We have to
come out to it on our own or we are not so much isolated as
lost. True separateness, true detachment, these are based on
choice, but often the psychiatrically sick has none. He *cannot*
connect, he *has* to be alone, even die. To offer him the status
of a pseudo-mystic is to offer him, instead of the richness of
an emotional life, a misplaced pride and a worthless glory.

Writing of schizophrenics, the American psychoanalyst John
Rosen affirms this: 'The ringside seats that they have had to
the pyrotechnics of the unconscious are hardly compensation
for the suffering schizophrenics have experienced.'[9]

Let us not worship nor absolve the schizophrenic. Instead,
let us offer him settings and environments in which he can
test out the validity of given health or wholeness for *him*. This
may not be enough. Some kind of therapy most probably must
be added to break the hermetic seal of the real self, but apart

[8] Colin Wilson, *The Outsider*.
[9] J. N. Rosen in *Direct Analysis*.

from Direct Analysis (Rosen's rate of success is marvellously high), I know of none that is consistently successful.

The aim of all therapy should be the return of the individual to himself. We are all inborn geniuses in hiding. Every one of us has it in him to do whatever has to be done. The potential of the least of us would obliterate the achievements of the most. The therapist needs to show his patient he has nothing to give that his patient does not already have for himself.

The most meaningful thing a therapist can do for his patient, at the right moment, is to change places.

My highest value, right now in my life, seems to be my own sense of reality. This is probably because I felt so unreal, schizoid, for so long. When I feel most real to myself, the world does too. And when I feel real I flow, I go with my tide, *the* tide, and then the inner and the outer are connected, move as one.

To speak of the Meaning of Life has no meaning to me. Life just is. But the meaning of life to me, that has meaning. It means more life, life squared, cubed, extended and enhanced. Nietzsche called it increasing one's palpitations.

There are certain situations in which this sense of reality becomes for me very strong. One of these is when someone is 'working' in a Growth centre workshop.

Growth centres, so far in this country, have had poor publicity. Naturally, since they are an innovation, English people treat them with suspicion. As for the press, they have treated them sensationally, concentrating on the aspects of touch and sensory awareness. That is their bias; they want to sell their publications. I have mine, for I want to sell the whole Growth movement. But gently.

In Growth centres 'work' takes place in groups of between about six and sixteen people. This in itself represents a resurrection of the ancient method of curing the sick before the whole tribe. The work is varied, but in all cases is geared to revealing and dispersing the distorting patterns of behaviour and experience that prevent us from being fully what we are,

24

and entering into total relationship with the environment, including that part of it that is other people. To do this, feelings have to be reached, because it is feelings that contain the dynamic energy to break the patterns.[10] This is where the methods score over traditional verbalized therapy.

Nothing can be done about these patterns without the energy of body, emotions, and mind combined. Worst of all are the obsessional neuroses that feed on their own self-consciousness. Where one of these fails to disperse only the force of emotional energy and thrust can shift it into insignificance. Full of importance, these neuroses stand guard before our hearts. Only by shifting our centre of gravity from *cerebrum* to *Kardia* will we feel what it is to be fully alive and whole.

Merely thinking about our state of being leads to nothing. Hope springs from the eternal centre that lies in the heart of every man. Whilst there's life there's hope because hope is life. Hope is the voice of life. And life lies in our hearts; death, as something separate from life, is but an idea in our heads.[11]

In Encounter groups people tell each other what they see in each other, as openly, directly and honestly as they can. These features swell as time goes on. Before long most false moves and phoney presentations are spied by someone. This way everyone becomes more real. Lies, masks, roles, pretences, drop away. What is left? Usually, raw feeling. The feelings that, rather than emerge, kept all those falsities going. Then the real work starts – letting the feelings flow, washing away the blocks, the emotional, the psychological and the physical that mirror and coalite with one another. Whenever this happens my heart wells up, my sense of reality takes a leap, and I feel highly alive, in a way that I sense I am meant to at all times. I am aware of my body, of every detail of what is happening before me, taking place in a crucible of quiver-

[10] And it is feelings, in the event, that give us faith: in life, in ourselves. Gurdjieff said (according to de Hartmann) that faith is the knowledge of feeling. This knowledge burns like a bright light in the crises of life. See T. de Hartmann, *Our Life with Mr Gurdjieff*.

[11] See Norman O. Brown, *Life Against Death*.

ing life. No matter what the feeling being shown – anger, love, fear, grief, desire, I always experience great joy.

As Beckett says, 'First dirty, then make clean.'

At the root of the whole movement is the drive to know what and who we are, and to *be* that, as the first requisite of change. If I deny my anger, how can I be rid of it, or change? My denial is itself a holding on.

Every block has a physical translation. Our bodies are the shape of our consciousness. Our energy flow, and what prevents it, are statements of our relationship with the world and ourselves. Our bodies continually speak to us. All we have to do is decode. When my feet tingle I need to take a walk. When my hands get cramp, I am blocking violence. When my throat is sore, I need to breathe differently, or stop smoking a while. Tightness in my chest means I need to open up, let go more, let it fly. When I bite my lip I am talking too much. And so on. Most people have pelvic blocks, due to guilt about sex. Many have body/mind blocks, part of the modern schizoid split, due to cutting off from painful feelings, aggravated by social and cultural emphasis on the hegemony of the head.

In a Bioenergetic workshop a trained leader locates these blocks and attempts to loosen them. Usually manipulation leads to a release of damned-up emotional energy, often related to a past experience of a particularly painful kind. In fact the spontaneous release of feeling associated with a past memory seems to refute at once the total rejection of traumata by Fritz Perls. Through the release of blockaded feeling in the workshop setting, we discover experientially that our catastrophic expectations about releasing our feelings upon the world and others are either groundless or obsolete. The child begins to relax his hold on the man. The man, for an instant, shakes himself free, casts around, and, very often, laughs from his guts.

So much has happened since those days of imposition. So much water under the bridge and yet no way round was found. Out of an experience the way is discovered. It is through. Laughter comes. Relief, joy, amazement, wonder, feeling free.

26

It does not last of course. The forces of constraint and habit are long-standing and strong. But the experience points the way, not merely cerebrally as under hallucinogens, but for the whole person, for every cell. Workshops do not deal in magic. What they do is to make manifest.

In a Gestalt workshop emphasis is on the here-and-now; on owning what we are *in toto*. I come to see that nobody does anything to me. I do it all to myself. You do not make me angry. At most you put me in touch with my own anger, which probably does not belong against you, but is stored up anger I have been afraid to express. The games people play, both with themselves and with others, are uncovered in increasing layers of subtlety and sophistication. I discover my own boundaries. I begin to take full responsibility for myself; for every movement of my body, every gesture, every thought and feeling. I own my experience from moment to moment, and I become aware of what it is, and its statement of what I am. I do not *have* thoughts, feelings, hands, stomach, back, penis, pains; I *am* these things, these parts of myself, and what they say is as much testimony of me, Michael Barnett, as any of these or any other words I offer to the world as exosmotic expression of my existence.

Through workshops of this kind I have opened up a lot. I am more direct – outflow; and I am less defensive – inflow. I leave myself alone more; that is, I trust myself more, trust more those parts of me I believed I always needed to control if they were not to wreak havoc with my life. Since this has led to some integration I am less at war with myself. I can live with myself far more comfortably even when things seem to be going badly, or painfully. I am no longer (very) afraid of myself, whereas once I lived in almost continual fear of myself. I am usually aware of what I am feeling, and mostly I am able to risk expressing those feelings directly. As a result of my experimentation I have come to believe that the best thing I can do for others as well as for myself is, on most occasions, to be myself and express myself honestly; that is, make known my feelings even if they do seem hurtful or negative. For it seems that whenever I do this – and there are many

27

other benefits too – there is, amongst other reactions, a huge sense of relief. This is because, in any case, we can never wholly hide our feelings. I might smile at you and speak honeyed words, even move to please you, but if in my heart I feel anger or hostility or dislike, you are going to know about it. My true feelings will radiate out from me, and if you are normally sensitive you will experience them. Consequently, when we are likeable to someone we do not like we are placing them in a double-bind. That is, we are sending them out two sets of contradictory messages. The effect of this can be immeasurably devastating. It also leads to a quite unnecessary confusion of what is.

Honesty is satisfying, even a joy. Truth is the leading voice of love – real and ultimate love. Simulated love can be a penance and arthritic. It is often without value. And it can be a violation. D. H. Lawrence saw love as a deliberate principle as 'an unmitigated evil'. Yes, distrust the love children : spite and hate are at hand. True love is expressed with truth, through truth. Out of my truth comes freedom : mine from pretence, yours from uncertainty and double-binds.

Today we live in an age of diplomacy and hypocrisy. Our social lives are shot through with deceit and deviation. Honesty is not rewarded, mystification is. It is implied, everywhere, that the survival of our society depends upon individual concealment and pretence.

Freedom, truth, reality, love : these are concomitants. They are also big abstract words, puffs if we are not careful. Nevertheless I hold that the first step to freedom is to speak the truth. With the truth felt, known and expressed, we gain a sense of own reality. In sharing that truth with others we show them love, and our respect.

I can remember the occasion when my wife Pamela told me she no longer loved me. This came at a time I believed her love for me to be vital, something without which I could not survive. But there it was, confronting me, the truth. And I can recall now the enormous sense of relief I felt. For I had guessed as much in my heart, and so had fought hard against it becoming the truth confirmed. Now I needed to fight no

28

more. I could let go, and so my anxiety went. I had the truth, and still I was alive.

Also through Growth groups I discovered the extent to which I was cut off from my body, and from my deep feelings; I became vividly aware of my need to perform – and dominate through star performance; of my difficulty in letting others have their feelings, especially when those feelings were 'negative', or about me, without feeling moved to change them, or soothe. I learnt these things, not with my head but with my whole self, so that in experiencing myself in action in these ways, I changed. Analytical interpretations force me, by contrast, to step out of my reality in order to think about them. This is the process of 'mind fuck'.

In a workshop[12] I relived my birth. I went through the struggle again, the fight to get out, felt my infant indomitability in the face of post-natal traumas (or impactive experiences). As a result of these re-enactments my chest, which had been constricted, as if frozen midway in a breath, for as long as I could remember, despite various attempts to flex it, relaxed at last – and has stayed so. Such things are very possible in these groups. I have seen people change drastically in their physical appearance : bodies straighten, humpbacks vanish, masks melt, faces completely alter, as there is a *seeing* by the whole organism, as opposed to a mere ideational understanding in the mind.

In another workshop[13] I became aware of the bands of iron I had placed around my neck in order to cut off my own sound : the sound of my real self. Slowly and deliberately I went through the fantasy of removing these one by one. When I had snapped the last one I leapt into the air, did a somersault in the air – something I had never even attempted, let alone accomplished, before – and soon after my voice began to emerge from my belly, no longer from my throat, and in my belly it remains.

On another occasion,[14] in psychofantasy, the bird in me

---

[12] With Denny and Leida Yuson.
[13] With Paul Lowe, now Ananda Teertha.
[14] In a workshop run by my friend and colleague, Jacob Stattman.

that wants to fly, and can fly, took off from its gilded cage
where I had lodged it, so that I jack-knifed ten feet into the
air, came down unhurt, and proceeded to draw out of my
anus the gelatinous accumulation of learning in my head, ending up so much in my body that I felt I had no head at all –
the Zen 'on-being-without-a-head' experience. Absolutely
beautiful. And quite terrifying. In another workshop[15] I went
into my fear, in and in, and found on the other side a state
of great and real joy. I find that feeling more and more often
now, for longer and longer.

The last words of *Nijinsky's Diary* read :

'My little girl is singing : "Ah ah ah ah." I do not understand
its meaning, but I feel what she wants to say. She wants to
say that everything . . . is not horror but joy.'[16]

This is frequently my transient but unmistakable experience
in workshops. Each time less transient. Each time more con-
tagious, more transferable to the whole world.

And in workshops, often enough, I have experienced in me
the snake that paralyses. My snake. Me. Most of us have
such a creature, only usually we project it on to others, or call
it convention, or society, or propriety. 'We kill the better half
of ourselves every day to propitiate them,' said G. B. Shaw,
meaning by 'them' the good citizens, the proper people. But
it is for our own sake we do it, not theirs, to save ourselves
from being what we are, and bringing down upon ourselves
the wrath of others. We want to feel safe, liked, accepted.

The fight is always with the self. It is the fight between
growth and embeddedness, between risk and safety, between
independence and social security, between self-support and
environmental support. As with the saint, every moment is a
moment of crisis in this struggle.

To 'work' in a Growth workshop is to be involved totally in
some individual exploration in this group setting, usually with
with only the group leader as facilitator, companion or guide,

---

[15] Also with Jay Stattman.
[16] See Bibliography.

into an area of feeling or blocked expression previously avoided. To work here is to penetrate one's own defences.

When this happens successfully the person working glows with his own life. He is fluid and flexible and for a while is no longer at war with himself, because he has given up the struggle to avoid a slice of his own reality. It is like finding you have been hovering over the earth, and now you have come down to it, merged with it, and the earth is both the earth and yourself. There is something mystical about these experiences. One becomes far more oneself at the very same time as he flows with the whole universe. I have felt this equally in Growth groups, in deep meditation, and in intense moments of communication. Paradoxically, the more one lets go of oneself, the more one becomes oneself. By trying to preserve oneself one limits oneself, for I cannot preserve myself, but only an image of myself, which is bound to be far less than what I am. By letting go of myself I can become myself. But this is hard to do deliberately. The logic of false preservation is powerful. There is a higher logic that can supersede it, but it takes some reaching. In the meantime we have to be tricked into it, or thrust into the experience of it by another. This is one of the truths at the root of the therapeutic relationship. At times we can do nothing on our own. Our very attempts to break out of our own patterns are part of our fabric of patterns. Gurdjieff, perhaps the mage of the age,[17] always maintained that the individual man was powerless to save himself. He *had* to have a certain amount of help from outside – from someone who *knew*.

Whenever I am present at someone's flood of feeling in a workshop I feel the warm flow of life and love in me too. And I always have the most tender and loving feelings for that person. When I am working *myself*, and in the aftermath, my sense of reality is so powerful that I become afraid, begin to wonder if I can bear it, though what that means I do not know, for who is the 'I' that cannot bear it, and what is 'it' that I cannot bear?

[17] Although his notions of control seem antipathetic to my sense of the rightness of the Tao, or natural way.

31

As Rilke puts it in the first *Duino Elegy* :

> For Beauty's nothing
> but beginning of Terror we're still just able to bear,
> and why we adore it so is because it serenely
> disdains to destroy us. Every angel is terrible.
> And so I repress myself, and swallow the call-note
> of depth-dark sobbing.[18]

Paradoxically, the only way of finding out about ourselves is to allow ourselves to fall into unknown territory. For most of us, all we know about ourselves is our patterns, the familiar ways in which we behave. This is a pittance of our potential. It is hard to escape the clutches of our behavioural systems and reach the richness of our being. This is partly because the part of us that has to let go of ourselves is the part of ourselves that we would lose if we did so. That part has no taste for suicide.

Yet there is no way of finding out about ourselves other than by falling into ourselves.

Meister Eckhart, founder of German mysticism, had this to say :

'If thou could naught thyself for an instant, less than an instant I should say, all that this is itself would belong to thee.'

R. D. Laing, modern mystic, like it or not, writes :

'True sanity entails in one way or another the dissolution of the normal ego, that false self competently adjusted to our alienated social reality : the emergence of the 'inner' archetypal mediators of divine power, and through this death a rebirth, and the eventual re-establishment of a new kind of ego-functioning, the ego now being a servant of the divine, no longer its betrayer.'[19]

[18] *Duino Elegies.*
[19] *The Politics of Experience.*

Or if you prefer Jesus:

'He that findeth his life shall lose it: and he that loseth his life for my sake shall find it.'

Jung, much influenced by the East, wrote in his way of the same experience, of the ego being replaced, without the connotation of being deposed; of an invisible centre taking over, of life becoming, 'it lives me'.

But how to let go? Zen Buddhism laughs at attempts to achieve *satori*, or *nirvana*. There is no way in which this can be done. Nothing can be done to make this happen. Not even nothing. Letting go has to take place naturally, of its own accord.[20]

Laughter, bowling out of a person in a Growth group as he or she *sees* reality, sees the absurdity of the games played to avoid this reality, for years upon years, this laughter *is* Zen, *is satori*. In these groups rubbish is being cleared away, dammed-up emotions let loose, the body freed, the mind freed, so that real living in the instant, the Zen experience, can happen. When it does, it is always beautiful.

Ra! Ra! Ra! The dithyrambic me. Encounter is playing the game of playing no more games. Then you have to throw away that game. It's a ladder you climb, then you kick the ladder away.

The ladder image. Or the Indian rope trick. Here is the end of Wittgenstein's *Tractatus Logico-Philosophicus*:

'My propositions are elucidatory in this way: he who understands me finally recognizes them as senseless, when he has climbed out through them, on them, over them. (He must so to speak throw away the ladder, after he has climbed up on it.) He must surmount these propositions, then he sees the

[20] Herrigel, in *Zen in the Art of Archery*, tells compellingly how he 'learned' to let go the arrow without willing it, without making the decision to let go, so that in the end the arrow was shooting itself. The Zen instruction on how to paint bamboos is similar: paint bamboos for ten years; become a bamboo, then just paint.

c

world rightly. Whereof one cannot speak, thereof one must be silent.[21]

Here is Beckett in *Watt* :

'What was changed . . . was the sentiment that a change . . . had taken place. What was changed was existence of the ladder. Do not come down the ladder, Ifor, I haf taken it away. This I am happy to inform you is the reversed metamorphosis. The Laurel into Daphne. The old thing where it always was, back again.'[22]

Another ladder is the spinal column in the mapping of Kundalini yoga. From primitive energy to cosmic consciousness. I shall have more to say about this later.

How far is the ladder of the Human Potential movement adequate? How far can it take us? Each method contained in it is limited. Each is a rung. Together they lead somewhere positive, towards freedom. But there is no 'cure' here yet. It is only a beginning, a rattling at the door. Janov, who discovered Primal therapy, claims his method is the only cure for neurosis. A fanciful claim. If he were right it would mean only his patients had ever been cured. No one else. Not even me. Imagine. But Janov's statement is self-fulfilling, for he defines as free from neurosis that state his patients are in after his therapy. So all he is saying is : no other method achieves what my method achieves. Well and good, probably. But do we all aspire to that state?

Any claim to have found *the* cure, or *the* anything come to that, is fraught with danger because it heads pell-mell for mechanism. For if we are all to be cured the same way we become merely interchangeable therapeutic units. Time and again innovators destroy the freedom and life of their inventions through their attempts to institutionalize and impose. Perhaps they wish to live on through the corpses of their systems. Through *their* attempts at deification, *we* suffer reification, time and again.

Like the rest of us in the Humanistic Psychology movement, Janov needs to be wary of *hubris*. For *hubris* is always blind.

[21, 22] For details, see Bibliography.

In men this blunder still you find,
All think their little set mankind.[23]

The aims and methods of both Encounter and Primal therapies are compensatory. Each age eventually throws up in
opposition what is missing from the culture. Lacking today are
honesty, directness, openness, silence, natural relationship with
the universe, emotional and physical identity. This new movement is an attempt to redress the balance.[24]

This heightened sense of reality, experienced in Encounter
groups when feelings run high, and bodies come alive, is

[23] Hannah More.

[24] The two main Growth centres in London are Kaleidoscope and
Quaesitor, both of which the writer is associated with. Each offers a
highly varied programme designed to help persons to grow and to become more aware and therefore more real. The literature available is
limited. On Encounter, the best book of an indifferent bunch is Bill
Schutz's *Here Comes Everybody*. Unfortunately, at the time of writing,
it is not yet published in this country. Schutz's book *Joy* is, but this is far
more limited in scope, and does not reflect, as the other does, what the
movement is trying to do in the mode of writing.

The definitive books on Gestalt are by Fritz Perls. *Gestalt Therapy
Verbatim*, which consists of taped talks and workshop extracts, is not
only full of flashing insights and a highly fresh awareness, but also in-
spiringly alive. Perls' autobiography, *In and Out the Garbage Pail*,
ignores all literary canons, is a complete hotchpotch of reminiscences
and observations, and yet succeeds, at least for me, in being quite
beautiful. Other books on Gestalt appear in this book's bibliography.

Bioenergetics derives from the work of Wilhelm Reich. His pupil,
Alexander Lowen, has written a number of books on body-oriented
therapy, the best in my opinion being *The Betrayal of the Body*. This
is a highly perceptive commentary on the schizoid state, one of the
malaises of the age. A little-known book, *The Puzzled Body* by the late
Caron Kent, can also be recommended. Only two books have appeared
so far on Primal therapy, both by Arthur Janov. Both are worth reading,
though I much preferred the first, *The Primal Scream*. The second is
an attempt at a justification that I do not consider necessary. And
besides, I think it fails. The book is called *The Anatomy of Mental
Illness*. Details of all books mentioned in this footnote, together with
others, are to be found in the bibliography.

Finally, in this note, I wish to point out that the descriptions in this
book of workshops and the various techniques employed in them are not
only personal but also highly rudimentary.

matched for me, curiously enough, when instead of identifying with my feelings, and letting them flow, I look into them and see through them, and reach a realm of calm detachment beyond.

When I reach this state everything I do and identify with in the world seems absurd. I see that whatever I do to correct or redress is simply setting up a counter-force perpetuating the whole mad whirligig, the everlasting seesaw : more of this, so more of that and less of this, so less of that and more of this and so on *ad infinitum*. I see that by attempting to rectify, I am caught up with the object, and to an extent trapped. I see then quite clearly the meaning of the Zen *koan*[25] which runs : How to get the goose out of the bottle? The answer? There, it is out! In other words, I can solve every problem that exists out there *for myself*, simply by detaching myself from it.[26]

To reach this state of detachment, or *moksha*, is the aim of all yoga, and the essence of individual Hinduism. From this valuation of the world, 'Passion, the voracious one, the wicked' becomes the enemy. That is what the Bhagavad-Gita says. The Gita is the handbook of Hinduism, equivalent to a merger, say, of the Bible, Pooh Bear, and Aesop's Fables. Hundreds of thousands of Hindus know it by heart. With an eighty per cent national illiteracy, perhaps this is not surprising, but that is another story. The Gita also says :

'If a man meditates on the objects of sense, attachment to them arises; from attachment desire is born; from desire anger is produced. Through anger comes bewilderment, through bewilderment wandering of the memory, through confusion of the memory destruction of the intellect, through the destruction of the intellect he is destroyed.'

---

[25] A *koan* is a Zen problem designed to help the adept towards enlightenment, more through grappling with it than solving it.

[26] And also solve, I am beginning to suspect, every problem (pseudo-problem) that exists *in here*, in myself. I detach myself from these by going with the flow, instead of trying to stabilize the everlasting cognitive seesaw. This entails a move in my centre from head to belly.

Catholicism could hardly have put it more uncompromisingly.

As ultimates these statements from the Gita may or may not be true, but as intellectual guides to controlled living I regard them as highly dangerous. They seem to set up conflicts: head against heart; will against nature. There is in them, as there is in my experience in Hinduism, too much striving.

Compare the Zen:

'Drinking tea, eating rice, I pass my time as it comes; looking down at the stream, looking up at the mountains, how serene and relaxed I feel indeed!'[27]

If the detachment experience is to be real and natural it must come of its own accord, without striving. Many of us gain glimpses and then try to hold on to what we see, which involves unnatural striving.

The principles of Kundalini yoga may help to illustrate what I mean.

According to this yogic method there are seven *chakras*, or organic centres, each corresponding to a different form of life, or energy. Actually and symbolically these centres are located along the spine. The first is at its base and consists of primitive energy. The levels then move up through the sexual, anger, affection, communication, intuition, to cosmic consciousness.[28]

Fundamental to this principle of development, or personal evolution, is the notion that no level or *chakra* can be skirted or skipped. The symbol is in fact a sleeping serpent coiled at the base of the spine. It cannot reach its ultimate height at the top of the head without moving through intermediate levels. In other words we have to move through emotional expressions of energy completely before we can reach true intuition and then effortless cosmic consciousness.

But as we grow we can get thrown up at times into a higher

[27] D. T. Suzuki.
[28] This is highly simplified; a bit like saying cricket is a game played with a silly mid-on.

level, even unto the seventh. This is so peaceful, even blissful, that we often try to remain there, prop ourselves up there falsely. This is sure to fail. It is the kind of thing that happens often enough with cannabis and LSD. Exponents fight to stay with the experience they gain, but the uncleared emotional levels will not be gainsaid. This accounts for the viciousness that appeared under the gentle veneer of many of the love children in the experimental drug era of the sixties. I distrust at once all those who profess to love everybody, who preach love as a way of life *at once*.

Apart from through drugs, and on other random and disparate occasions, I have felt this cosmic detachment a number of times when with two persons I met through the setting up of PNP : Mike Williamson and John O'Shea.

When I first met Mike, right back at the very beginning of the PNP enterprise, he was an advertising executive with a promising future, but with grave doubts about the whole social value system of which he was a part. His doubts took the form of a continuous debate : weighing, thought, reweighing, thought. It wasn't long before Mike dropped out and took the inner and the alternative trips. But still the debates continued. This unending mental hopscotch apart, Mike had a great deal of energy, insight and patience, all of which proved invaluable to PNP. Along with David Eddy he did more than anyone else to help Pam and me establish PNP. He saw dozens of people and did not stint his time.

John O'Shea had his own style. There he was at our door one night, out of the blue, from across the seas, still and dapper and smiling, with mystery surrounding. His pain showing. Pam and he and I, we made music that night, the way it is with people sometimes, when their separate boundaries fade, even go. Such experiences, increasingly frequent these days, perhaps herald a new age.

His seal on it came a day later : a postcard of the Queen in full regalia : gold and blues, in Technicolor; on its back the message : 'Thanks for a lovely high !' That picture; I can't work out why it was so right, but right it was, exactly. Perfect. John had an ear for such things.

He and Mike Williamson met at our flat, for the first time I think, Christmas Eve, 1969. We spent the night hours together, the four of us, visiting lands of terror and wonder, crossing thresholds of consciousness, feeling the pain of seeing the games we played. What a night. Dawn came with us limp, with me suffering myself as never before. We had spent a month on a raft on the high sea and I had not liked what I had done. Without Shem, then twenty-one months, to guide me and hold me, I might have died with the pain.

Out of that night came much. One thing – John joined Mike in his flat and together they began to make a series of *total investigations* : meditation, Zen, Krishnamurti, Don Juan the Yaqui Indian shaman,[29] etc.

No half measures here. Books were sold, hifi, tv, records too (though both kept their guitars, which they played beautifully). Furniture was practically eliminated : white walls, a round low table, sets of planks around it for chairs; that was all for a while. The plank sets were in threes : one horizontal, one vertical, the third oblique, a strut. On these they would sit for hours looking into their experience, in a silence broken only by a flash or a jest and its laughter, or to the tune of Mike's sometimes hilarious, occasionally tedious, articulated interior debates.

Soon they formed the Psychenautics Institute, for journeys into inner space. Its chief activity was looking into things, intently, with such valour and energy, that their essential nothingness was exposed. Emotions, pains – these were not to be expressed but probed, peeled, broken up, unravelled, dissolved, and thereby true detachment from them reached. Through things to no-things into all things. The mystical experience. Into the nothingness in which everything is.

There with them, at times, I would have this vision, I would know its truth. I would see the world outside in which I lived, that is to say I would see my living that life, as totally insane. All that getting and spending, that fuss and flurry, the incessant seesaw, manipulation and control, attack and defence, the pursuit of an empty plenty, the 'riding an ox in search of an

[29] See the books by Carlos Castaneda listed in the Bibliography.

ox' – so futile and ridiculous. How could I do it? Mad, mad. Sitting, silence, stillness, these were perfect, exquisite, this was It. This, at first painful and then breathtakingly rich and simple, sitting and experiencing the flow of life through one-self, waiting for nothing, without wanting, just flowing, sensing, feeling, thinking, just that. And John and Mike and I would become almost one.

But before long I would experience a longing for *maya*, for the 'big, booming, buzzing confusion'. I wanted to get back to where the action was, the daft chasing and the tragic suffering. It had been nice, my mini-Nirvana, but I did not wish to remain. Either *I* wasn't ready, or *it* wasn't right. My friends, Mike, John, Pam, they would be disappointed in me. But to stay would have been to suffocate. Not from what was there, but from what was not.

As far as I know the Psychenautics Institute never had more than two full members: Mike and John – despite a series of weird, elaborate and intriguing notices placed in publications varying from *Time Out* to *The Times*. This wasn't surprising really. Those who would have qualified would never have replied, in my opinion. Novitiates were offered, but Mike and John, from what I saw, were not gentle teachers and it would have taken a brave person to run the gauntlet of apprentice-ship. Still, I don't think Mike and John minded unduly. There were honorary members, like Pam, who enjoyed them, whom they enjoyed; they were not alone. At times it was intimated to me I only had to ask, to be elected. Given the stringency of membership, I suppose this was flattering, but I was not tempted. It was not my way.

Besides, I could not see them as teachers, for me. In Kun-dalini yoga terms I felt they had not worked through their *chakras*, or else they were doing it in a way that did not lead me to reach out for them. And it bugged me, the way Mike angrily denied his anger, competitively disowned his com-petitiveness, defensively disclaimed his defensiveness. There is little doubt my style – angry, arrogant, provocative – helped evoke all this; nevertheless it was in him, it was in him as mine was in me.

40

At Mike's centre I was sure – I am still sure – there was a core of stillness, strength and creativity, out of which would come at times a verbal brilliance, an astonishing creative wit, but around this was darkness then denied.

John? He seemed mostly on his proper way, in touch undoubtedly with a new and more exalted way of seeing. But he had not yet tied up the old. A bird can fly, but first it must be hatched. John would say his stumbling block was survival. How to do so in this warped and cut-throat world whilst remaining true to his higher self? But as with the rest of us, John's stumbling block lay not in the world but in himself. He had not mastered, but lost, the art of the ordinary. Like India, he had not married up contemplation and action. Perhaps that is why, when he went there, he disliked it so much.

In what I have written about my friends Mike and John, there may be a bias. For I have to confess to a running jealousy I had of them both, especially of Mike, around that time, on account of Pam, whose relationship with them was loving and fast and strong. I suffered from these bonds, was often jealous, even fiercely so, hated my jealousy, loved and hated the whole set up, loved Pam, loved Mike, hated him too, liked John a lot, hated him too, and what all that did to my judgement, God knows. Yet I do not admit to present prejudice, as I write, free of Pam emotionally as I am, and with much warmth in me for Mike and for John, but it might be there, oh yes.

Finally, and at last, on reality, I want to briefly mention two other kinds of occasion when I sense this strongly. The first is when I speak my truth when it is difficult to do so, when I affirm myself and in doing so put myself at risk, even if all I 'have' may go. The other is when I am 'in my body'; that is, actually experiencing it as it stands, moves, swings, one leg moving ahead of the other, my arms swinging, feeling the air, the air passing, my feet making growing contact with the ground. All this may be as nothing to many, but to someone like me who spent years cut off from his body it is a small miracle.

Let me give the last word on reality to that crotchety, pedantic old mage, Krishnamurti :

'Reality can be found only in understanding what *is*; and to understand what *is*, there must be freedom, freedom from the fear of what *is*.

'To understand that process there must be the intention to know what *is*, to follow every thought, feeling and action; and to understand what *is* is extremely difficult, because what *is* is never still, never static, it is always in movement. The what *is* is what you are, not what you would like to be; it is not the ideal, because the ideal is fictitious, but it is actually what you are doing, thinking and feeling from moment to moment.'[30]

What I am thinking right now is how little drug therapy is related to this valuation of reality. The purpose of most drugs used therapeutically is to hide reality, fog up what is. But what *is* remains, still the personal truth. Any therapy based on the fictions of sedation and neutralization can never cure. All they do is shore up a false reality that is existentially untrue.

It is true that many people may feel they would be happier with that than with a painful and perhaps seemingly hopeless reality. Just because I refuse to compromise with what I take to be the truth does not mean others should not.[31] I suppose. Yet I recoil from such a compromise on behalf of all men, with or without the right.

To choose drugs is to choose dependency. It removes us from ourselves. It shifts our centre from within to without. In a way it is like a tight marriage. With my spouse or my drug I become a pseudo-couple, and elude my personal freedom.

These unbearable and apparently hopeless realities, how do they arise? And how can they be dissolved?

The roots of a plant reach out for nutrition. Place the nourishment elsewhere and the roots change direction. From moment to moment they look after themselves. A hedgehog, sensing danger, curls up, unwinds when it is passed and walks on. It responds uninterruptedly to what *is*.

We are more complicated. We have developed minds that

[30] M. Lutyens (ed.), *The Penguin Kruishnamurti Reader*.
[31] What I *take* to be the truth is of course probably itself a compromise.

make something of our own experience, and impress conclusions about life on our future. Our past programmes us, willynilly. We cry, say, a hundred, a thousand, times as a child to no avail. So perhaps for a lifetime we cry out no more. We cease to ask for our needs to be met. We flee from danger, deep into ourselves, time upon time, until the moment comes when we batten down the hatches, perhaps never to re-emerge. We express anger, resentment, even gaiety and joy, and are bawled at, or belted for it time and again, so that we disconnect from these feelings, deny they exist. We are oppressed by a parent, even persecuted, and conclude that the world out there is against us, for ever. We never start afresh. We are prisoners of our past, of our memory. The child indeed is father to the man. Thought locks timelessly at a stroke. It assesses for ever, though the facts may have been fanciful and, besides, now obsolete.

Memory is a catastrophe. Escape from its grip is a prerequisite of spontaneous living. Our experiences are with us anyway, in our cells and fibres, in our very spontaneity. We do not need files, still less micro-clerks, summaries, articles of action.

For Freud, the neurotic was someone who was unable to escape from his past. The grip is the patterns of old habits, obsolete logic, and fear. We fear to let go of what we think we are, but what we are not. And what we fear is not the dark but what we are, and what we are has no fear of itself. Fear keeps us from no-fear. By fearing to feel we rob ourselves of experience. By failing to let go we rob ourselves of ourselves.

> In order to arrive at what you are not
> > You must go through the way in which you are not.
> And what you do not know is the only thing you know
> And what you own is what you do not own
> And where you are is where you are not.[32]

Habits, infantile logic and fear combine to convert us, freeflowing human beings, into scaffolding, fabrics of rigid inter-

[32] T. S. Eliot, East Coker, *Four Quartets.*

locking patterns. Freedom (and therapy) consists in dispersing these patterns.[33]

At least, since these patterns are mutually supporting, if we disperse one we can often disperse a whole bunch, making a rent, and even, with luck, finding the void.

Once in an Encounter group a woman was told by other members that they found her cold and aloof. She also had an overworked upper-crust accent. I asked her if she could imitate any other accent and she said, yes, she could do Yorkshire, where she was brought up. She continued talking, but with that dialect, and instantly her haughtiness and coldness vanished; she became soft and warm and friendly. The effect was so magical, and such a relief that the group just laughed, rolled about laughing. A whole set of patterns had disappeared.

Perhaps the dissolution of neurotic systems is part of the invisible logic behind the use of ECT, or electro-convulsive therapy.

The origins, and developmental logic, of this method are interesting.

'In 1935 von Meduna noted that schizophrenics did not commonly suffer from epilepsy, while epileptics had relative freedom from schizophrenia. On the basis of this observation, which later turned out to be incorrect, he decided to try the effects of a cerebral stimulant which was known to produce epileptic fits when given in toxic doses. He had accurately remarked the occasional improvement shown by the schizophrenic who was also epileptic, after a spontaneous fit. Accordingly, von Meduna injected cerebral stimulants intravenously, causing the patient greater and greater agitation as the level in the blood rose, until a fit caused loss of consciousness . . . probably no treatment has ever engendered so much fear in the hearts of those receiving it. One frivolous theory about its

[33] Few would question that the body has selective patterns based on needs, real or imagined, but ever fewer accept that the mind has selective patterns too, based on *its* needs. Moreover, the body would not claim that its correspondence with the universe was anything but subjective and transient, whereas the mind pretentiously believes all too readily that its selected material is objective, universal and timeless.

effectiveness was that it was so terrifying that even the psychotic would deny his symptoms to get off the treatment list. . . . In 1937–8 the method of producing fits by the brief passage of an electric current across the temples was introduced by Cerletti and Bini, and the treatment of psychosis by convulsions become at once less cumbersome and more humane.'[34]

David Cooper's account differs. According to him Cerletti discovered ECT in the abattoirs of Rome where he saw that in those pigs who did not die from electrocution, there were marked changes in behaviour.[35]

So there we have the infantile psychiatric logic that patterns treatment still today. Hays later goes on to say,

'[ECT] produces a transient memory difficulty which may upset a patient who is already concerned about himself and may feel that his memory is specially vulnerable; it is not infrequently followed by a severe headache which may last several hours; and it occasionally produces in patients a pronounced fear of the treatment that is unexplained and is out of all proportion to the triviality of the procedure.'

The whole tone of this passage reeks of dehumanization. We have a professional talking about patients from *his own* and not in the least from their point of view. Who is he, this purveyor of the treatment, to talk of 'the triviality of the procedure'? His whole approach is authoritarian and status ridden as he speaks of 'transient' memory loss, and 'upset' patients. Like most practitioners, he chooses to identify with his role rather than with his humanity. If the psychiatrist as subject could become, for a while, patient as object, his perspective would become radically changed.

I have met many people who have been treated with ECT. Few regard it with anything short of abhorrence. Most refuse to recall their experiences, which they have well buried. The mindless nature of the process apart, it represents an experience

[34] Peter Hays, *New Horizons in Psychiatry*.
[35] In *Death of the Family*.

of being treated as a *thing*. Man is the creature who has freedom, who is *aware*, at some level, of the existence of this freedom. Experiences where this is abstracted from him are always
nightmarish. Think back on your own.

Shock, when administered person to person, can be beneficial. The state of *existential* shock is a 'being' situation; that
is, one in which we become aware of our here-and-now reality,
and truth. I am grateful to those who, in my life, have spoken
to me straight, swept aside my mask, and reached me, so that,
for an instant, I became myself. Each time it was a kind of
satori, or moment of enlightenment. But volts through the head
when under sedation, where can be the learning, the 'seeing',
the flash of realization in that?

Patterns, on a social scale, take the shape of conventions,
traditions, institutions. These are the congealed habit patterns
of us all, and our ancestors. And yet they are not out there, in
the world, but in us. 'There is no such thing as the state'[36] –
there are only people acting repeatedly in certain patterned
ways. To believe in 'society', in 'conventions', as entities, is to
mystify oneself.

So that kind of psychiatry consists merely of modes of
thought and action shared by a set of specialists, plus public
collusion.

Psychoanalysis consists of the adoption by an intellectual
elite of the way a man named Freud conceptualized the world.
Each time a psychoanalyst places the Freudian meaning system
between himself and the world of experience, we have thought
instead of reality, life robbed of its blood. And of course
Freudianism is a 'total symbolic universe',[37] that explains
everything in terms of itself. For instance, any scepticism or
doubt about the meaning system is accounted for *by* the system
with the notion of 'resistance'.

Such a universe of meaning is lethal because it can lead to
the relinquishment of our separate freedom to experience the
world separately for ourselves. It is also seductive. The sociologist Peter Berger writes:

[36] W. H. Auden.
[37] The term is Peter Berger's. See *Social Construction of Reality*.

'The experience of conversion to a meaning system that is capable of ordering the scattered data of one's biography is liberating and profoundly satisfying. Perhaps this has its roots in a deep human need for order, purpose and intelligibility. However, the dawning recognition that this or any other conversion is not necessarily final, that one could be converted and re-converted, is one of the most terrifying ideas the mind can have.'[38]

How ironic that Freud's method, designed to free patients from their past, should itself become neurotic, that is, become a victim of historical rigidity!

My origins in practical psychiatry I have already described, but my predilection for studying others, their ways and their patterns, began much earlier. Perhaps I came out of the womb sizing everyone up. But I doubt it. I suspect I had a life of my own then and would have been content to live it. What happened next remains shrouded in mystery, though the curtains are opening. But how can I be sure that what I believe I discover is not my own invention? Perhaps I am hunting my own slipper in order to lose myself in the game. But my theory is this: I set my mind on studying my mother so that I could find out what she wanted, in order to give it to her, and so get back my own needs. Either I had to, in order to get it, or decided to, in case I did not. I do not know; it is all too easy to make her my scapegoat. Parents: it is always *their* fault. But I am sure that my relationship with her led to the hypertrophy of my middle eye – at the expense of the other two. Today I see people's patterns and existential choices like some see auras and others lives in palms.

By the age of four I was already beginning to live vicariously. Unable to flow with others, be simply with them, I watched them instead, and built my own world in my head. The trouble was that though part of it was real, product of middle-eye vision, part of it was not, but rather the issue of my own needs

[38] *Invitation to Sociology.*

and longings. It all mingled, until the truth was lost. And yet I knew I *saw*. What could I do? I had a gift, but could not trust it, for it had become adulterated.

Most of my life I have been schizoid. That is, not fully in touch with reality. I managed to build quite an effective false self and never once let it go until recently. Perhaps only then was I ready. This need to be ready for the truth is something I am too prone to forget when working with others on their development. On the other hand I believe in the ultimate strength of the life force in everyone. I assume that if that force can be contacted then the opposing forces of anti-life can always be overthrown. Self-destruction, in its forms in man, seems to me to be against nature. Of course in a sense, since this phenomenon is part of man, it is also part of nature, or the whole process. But it is based on a myopic view of survival, a 'what-we-have-we-hold' mentality. Growing involves risk on this crowded planet, the risk of competition, opposition, antagonism, pain. The logic of the constricting forces is – rather a cramped parody of life than take the risk of altogether perishing. But as soon as we identify with that *Weltanschauung*, or way of seeing the world, we pervert the life force, because that force is dynamic, it does not simply mean life, but more life, growth towards an inherent maximum. If we hold an amount of life still, in greed, in fear, in obstinacy, in perversity, we kill it, because we thwart its nature, and when nature is thwarted it does not mark time, for that is against its nature, but dies.

Somehow, schizoid, partly dead, or at least unreal, I managed to get on. In social terms, that is. A good degree, high success in business, and plenty of women, at least one I learnt the knack of intuiting their needs, and then providing them for my own ends.

Then in 1963 I began to come alive. I viewed my life with disgust. Where was I going? And what for? I was beginning to get in touch with my innate, as opposed to my social, reality. Almost nothing in my phrenetic life was giving me any real satisfaction. It would not do. Once I made contact with my own nature, everything was decided. That is to say, I would

48

follow my own nature. By following it the die would be cast.

But unreality, deceit, living the images others have of us and the image we have of ourselves, all these are not so easily sloughed off. Ramakrishna, the Indian mystic, used to tell the story of the man who kept saying that one day he would renounce everything and become a *sadhu*, a Hindu monk. One day his wife sneered at him and said to him he would never do it, he could only talk, whereupon the man slung a cotton towel over his shoulder and walked off for ever.

We cannot walk away from our past selves so easily. But at least I dropped out. I left a career and a steep salary behind, an extravagant existence, and my friends thought me brave. They were wrong. I had ceased, in some respects, going against my own nature, and that was easier than falling off a log.

But I did not yet know what it was I wanted to do. It took me another eight years to discover that. I was well hidden. I had been cowering, petrified, for more than thirty years. How could I expect myself to take courage in less than eight?

My initial decision was to become a writer. Imagine. *Deciding* to become a writer. Only hacks do that. Real writers write, like it or not. Here is Beckett talking to Georges Duthuit about the Dutch artist, Bram van Velde:[39]

B: The situation is that of him who is helpless, cannot act, in the event cannot paint, since he is obliged to paint. The act is of him who, helpless, unable to act, acts, in the event paints, since he is obliged to paint.
D: Why is he obliged to paint?
B: I don't know.

I sense Beckett speaks here of himself too. This is the working of nature: irresistible, indecipherable, inexplicable. It is the experience of nature acting and living through us in its proper way, so that we become our own shape.

I told as many people as possible of my new career. I would say, 'I am going to become a writer' in a tone that assured my

[39] Beckett & Duthuit, *Three Dialogues.*

listeners that it was only a matter of time before their shelves were lined with my books.

One of those I felt obliged to inform was an old friend of mine from Cambridge, whom I will call Mark. I had remembered him as reading English (it turned out to be History), and besides I had heard he was working for *The Times*, and that was literature, surely. Do I sound naïve? Well I was.

I gave him some coffee, settled him comfortably, and told him of the momentous decision. He arched an eyebrow and asked me, *why then was I not writing*? It had been several months since my decision, and I would like to have produced for him a couple of novels. As it was there was only a lame collection of maxims and observations carefully collated during this time and written in a variety of styles, all reminiscent of the eighteenth and nineteenth centuries, and none of them really mine, except one. Mark unerringly picked this one out and said he quite liked it, the rest he pronounced rubbish. I was hurt. I did not see that he had confirmed me, and waved away my phoniness. In a way, because these maxims were imitative, their importance for me was intense. Had I not sold myself out for them?

Recalling that day, I see how blind I was. Even then an essential part of me was far more interested in the fact that Mark, at the age of thirty-two, was still living with his mother, than in our discussion on my writing. I was blind, of course, because I did not wish to see. I did not wish to delve into others' lives, I wanted to become a writer. Had I not said so?

The fact is, I only wanted to become a writer as a way of symbolically filling up space, that is to say, time. Since I did not know who I was, and therefore what I wanted to do, how was I to live, to pass time? In addition, my brother had had a book published. This I had to equal; no, excel. Since, throughout my life, he would never let me join him, I had to beat him. Besides, I felt my father loved him more; he, the Jewish first-born, was favoured. I loved my father, and wanted his love, and so had to prove him wrong.

As you can see I belonged, like most of us, to my own history. Just as in detachment I see how my life activity is simply perpetuating the merry-go-round of futility and suffering, so from my original being I see how my inner activity is almost wholly devoted to offsetting past experiences, to settling accounts. This has to be finished, closure reached, or else its foolishness perceived, before we can get back to what we truly are, and act in accordance with our true nature. Or so it seems.

And so I went off to India to become a writer. I started at once, making notes as I travelled through Europe and the Middle East. This was the normal practice, was it not? But it was of no use to me. I can only write either as I see things or as I recall them at a point in time. Consequently I cannot edit or revise, I can only rewrite. I write now with the first draft of this book beside me, and I hardly glance at it. That first draft was written from the first completed book on PNP, without repeating a word. That first book was rejected in its entirety by me. Apart from others' criticism, within a month of its completion I could not bear it. In turn this book no doubt will be comprehensively repudiated.

In India I wrote my first half million words, most of which I scattered into the seas. I had a set of articles published, and paid for, by the *Hindustani Standard*. The editor of this esteemed publication glanced quickly at them, and within half a minute was handing me over the rupees. Only an Indian can grasp a nettle and place it between leaves. I lost the money at once, gambling it away in games of rummy played at a rupee a point. I played worse than I ever remember. It was obvious I wanted to lose.

Why? Because I felt I did not deserve to win. Those few articles, laboured over with love so long, were already to me so much worthless dust. (Besides, gambling is my weakness. Not, as with my father, with money usually. But with those I love.)

To end is to begin, to begin again. Gambling for high stakes, such as a friend or lover, always means an end, or a new beginning; that is, it always means a beginning. And that has been my chief motive : to begin again.

Sand

By summer 1966 Pam and I were in Japan, each of us working the ultimate in short time, the half-day week, *and* saving money.

For a while I spent the best part of my six and a half free days each week reading and writing, still pitifully believing in salvation through words. But I had to discover their limitations for myself. After all, in ten years prior to leaving England I had read perhaps fifty books all told. Now my rate was more like two hundred a year. There was quite a backlog, but at least, travelling, I did not have to keep abreast, not knowing the latest petitions for my time. Eventually my reading slowed down, but I kept writing, for this was part of a major project, only just beginning to emerge, to become free – to free myself, that is, from my past, and its hold on me through needs and compulsions that were once so great that they threatened to eat me up for ever. But a bird stirred and I heard.

I wanted to reach the state in which I was responding freshly, openly and with full awareness to each moment as it came. Project Demystification. Captain Michael Barnett: prepare for permanent *satori*.

I began some serious meditation in Japan, regularly each day for once. At the end of each session I would sit down at the typewriter and write an episode of a story *Snow*, about a man tramping endlessly through snowy wastes, missing nothing of his experience. Eventually he reaches a haven, an inn, alight but without persons. He eats and drinks, warms himself and sleeps. Next morning he is found, a hundred miles from anywhere, dead from exposure in the snow – but with a bottle of cognac in his hand.

52

As you can see, a *tour de force*. I have the scraps of it somewhere – the only relic of the half million words belonging to my Japanese period. Apart, that is, from a series of fierce and arrogant letters that appeared in the Tokyo press on the subject of God. Jesus himself could hardly have claimed to know more about it.

One day, floating about in the British Council library, stoned from having just read Beckett's *From an Abandoned Work* for the first time, I idly, as they say, picked a book off the shelves called *The Self and Others* by a psychiatrist called R. D. Laing. I was a bit behind the times, but there it was. I flicked through it, and was amazed to find in it such familiar figures to a man of letters like me as Genet, Dostoevsky, G. M. Hopkins, Nathalie Sarraute, not to mention friendly philosophers like Hegel, Sartre, Buber, Blake and Hsi Yun. I sat down and began to read it, and it slowly began to dawn on me that I had found home. Here was the definitive field, for it was about *me*, and it was about *others*, whom I had studied in my sly, subtle, avid, unavowed way for so long. Moreover, as I read I became bewitched by an entirely new experience. At times, instead of finding myself thinking *about* what I was reading, I discovered I was actually thinking *what* I was reading, so that the book and I in a way became one.

I wrote to the author, congratulating him if I remember rightly on his splendid effort, but putting him straight on one or two points where he had erred, and promising to look him up when I got back to London. When I did it was as a prospective patient, and it cost me twelve guineas.

I reached London in June of 1967 after a leisurely trip back from Japan through Ceylon, India, Afghanistan, Persia, Turkey and Greece. Then hop, hop, like a wallaby, through Corfu, Italy, Switzerland and France, and we were there.

It makes no difference : a day in the country, two weeks in Italy or Spain, four years in the East, with my first sight of a London bus or an Underground station my heart always lifts in gladness and love. I am a true Londoner.

I was back but I did not know what I would do. I had no plans, except for the vaguest ones concerning psychiatry. My old fields were finished for me and my writing was making nothing. Even if I sold the manuscripts I had humped back across half the world, it wouldn't keep us for long, nor at once.

Then there was my mother to look after. She had not been too well when I had left in '63, but the first time I saw her on my return I went away and sobbed. This poor brave staggering person racked by infinite degrees of pain. For years she had suffered from migraines, and then from Parkinson's Disease, gradually worsening. In '63, before I left, she had had a cancer operation, and now the creeping thing had returned. Yet daily she dragged and shuffled her way to the West End to work with her blind indomitability and sense of duty – which, combined, kept her going, and at the same time, I suspect, had brought about her downfall. Her iron will had killed her, just as then it was keeping her alive. When she died, nine months later, she at last let go, and I saw on her face, relaxed finally, what she looked like, what she *was*, behind her striving and her struggling.

I know all about that syndrome. It is in me. It is my left side. For years, with my mother's help, it tried to rule me, so that behind my rebelliousness was my fear of and dependence on others. Behind my revolt I did not belong to myself.

Slowly I began to swing over to my right. I use that hand more; I even began to write with it. My whole body straightened up from its long-standing heavy list to the left that caused such a strain upon my left leg muscles that they eventually collapsed in 1970 from trying to maintain a semblance of balance. During this shift from left to right, for a long while even my penis swung that way, hanging down on my right thigh; unless I began again to identify with my left characteristics, whereupon it would swing over and hang on to the left. Right now it hangs straight, and I feel straight, if not quite synthesized, left and right. For instance parts of this book have been written with one hand, parts with the other, and parts with both, direct on to the typewriter; as a way of getting all of me into the act.

54

Into my mother's home we moved, so that Pam could tend. I was moving all over, but did not know where to go. This set up a scratch squad of pains, all of which made me feel I was on my way out of the world – especially the one drilling definitively through my left side, into the open air.

Eventually I went to my GP for a checkup. Finding nothing he passed me on to a hospital for a head-to-toe examination. I was X-rayed on a spit, a criminologist's anatomy, and then sent away to grind and wait. Nothing was revealed. Finally there was a specialist willing to stick his rubberized finger up my anus and wiggle it around. He pronounced me fit and free of affliction.

Instantly my pains vanished. I had been convinced by experts that there was nothing there, why should my body go on sending me messages?

Every pain, strain, tension and tic is a message: direct and unambiguous. All we have to do is decode it. However, at that time my awareness had not reached such a high level of sophisfication, that is to say it missed the obvious.

So the battleground switched to my head. I could hardly think in an inch-straight line. Swirls and wiggles, screws and hop-o'-my-thumbs were all I could muster, as I ploughed on through Kierkegaard and Sartre, seeking my solution.

Finally I decided I would have to go and see R. D. Laing. I had followed up *The Self and Others* with *The Divided Self* and *The Politics of Experience*, recently out, and quite clearly the man knew more or less all the answers.

So I paid my twelve guineas and went. He was reassuringly substantial with his Scots accent and his brown corduroy jacket. His consulting room was like a Beckett set, *End Game* probably, and we sat in it whilst I spilled him out my woes and complaints. Mostly he listened, with an occasional query.

Later I listened to him tell me that he thought I had maybe lost touch with myself around the age of four or five, and that perhaps I should try to get back. LSD might help. I listened carefully, though part of me at that time did not want to get well, but to go on as I was, madly regarded; perhaps putting out an *œuvre* of insane, fantastically funny books.

But all things take their course. I remember little else Laing said. Perhaps he said little else. He spoke of a transparency of being, and I remember that I cleverly countered by saying that Sartre held consciousness and self-identity to be incompatible. Laing said Sartre could be wrong.

Of course. And so he is. But at the time this seemed an amazing possibility. With my head in my head, philosophy was truth, for me. Laing said he would write to me suggesting someone I might see on a regular basis. I should see that person and decide whether or not I wanted to work with him. If not I should get back to him, Laing, and he would suggest another.

I waited for what seemed a long time. I was impatient to be cured. Then my GP who had arranged the appointment heard. I asked him what Laing had said. He wriggled, and said he could not tell me, it would be unprofessional. The letter was on his desk. I read it upside down. Back to front, upside down, it is all the same to me. Laing had written that I was one of an uncommon breed of people who changed radically every seven years, causing themselves and others great upheavals.

That was nice to know. Of course Laing could be wrong. But, looking back, the fact was he was about right. The number 7 haunts my life, and now here it was again. It is my *karma*, this number, and I am to get beyond it.

But I was annoyed. This practice amongst the medical profession of talking together *about* patients rather than to them – it's disrespectful. And it encourages dependency. Moreover, all my life I have had this fantasy that I am equal to anyone. I don't remember being overawed by any person for more than ten minutes. By then I have seen their pathology and written their supremacy off.

In the meantime I was scouting around, prior to making the move into psychiatry. A new friend, David Eddy – my brother's wife's sister's husband's brother, believe it or not –

suggested I look up a few people like Leon Redler and Aaron Esterson.

Leon, an existential anti-psychiatrist and a friend of Laing's, was a short, sparkling man with a happy, flashing mind. I liked him a lot. He made several suggestions, but none of them clicked. Aaron, who wrote *Sanity, Madness and the Family* with Laing, and *The Leaves of Spring*, agreed to see me at once. In a sense it was he who set the whole ball rolling.

Silt

Aaron listened carefully while I told him about myself and what I wanted to do. He gave me space. Also he watched me intently, so that with space and attention I felt very real. I can recall the sense of it today, along with other times when I have been granted both at once.

He listened whilst I told him that I believed the schizoid syndrome represented the beginnings of a mutation in man. He was amused and said there was no room in orthodox psychiatry for a man with views like that.

Of course, being schizoid still, I was trying to justify myself. Also I was confused between self-consciousness and self-awareness. The first interferes, inhibits, judges. The latter is the transparency that Laing had talked of, a simple watching, an awareness of what one is. Awareness does not spoil, it moves one into new reaches of being because it sees what is and absorbs it so that change *comes* about, but it not *brought* about. To bring about change in oneself is to set up conflict. It is the difference between giving up smoking by resolution, and simply stopping. The first, in my belief, solves nothing, but simply switches the war elsewhere. The second, when it happens, just happens naturally, changing what *is*.

Still Aaron was disposed to help. 'Why not try and get a job at the "Q" Hospital?' he said. He knew the matron there and would recommend me.

I went to see her and got on well, though later this changed. I started work there soon after as an Auxiliary Nurse at £9 a week.

The 'Q' Hospital sits on the edge of a heath. It houses anything up to fifty patients, all of whom are classified as neurotic.

58

There are few restrictions on them, and they are allowed to come and go more or less as they please. They are strongly encouraged to go home, or elsewhere, at the weekends. Nights out in the week are frowned on, but allowed if the reasons are good.

The patients form a therapeutic community, that is to say they have some responsibility in running their own lives whilst there, including helping in the day-to-day mechanics of the establishment. There are a number of expectations put upon them; the pressure if these are not met is applied sometimes directly, at other times subtly. For instance, refusal to carry out prescribed duties, or remaining in bed all day, are seen as evidence of deterioration, or at least of lack of co-operation in their own cure (as institutionally defined), and as a result the right of community membership is called into question. This sort of manipulation is seen as appropriate, since it reflects reality, where reality is defined as the way of things *out there*. It is prudent, therefore, as a patient, not to become too ill, otherwise you are liable to be transferred to a more rigorous establishment commensurate with the intense nature of your disturbance.

Patients at the 'Q' are not given ECT or confined in any way, and rarely given drugs. Instead each sees a psychotherapist two or three times a week, and works with him or her towards cure. In addition, and as ancillary aids, the patients attend regular community meetings of all patients, nurses, and the current community doctor. Also, there are further divisional meetings of groups of patients and nurses only.

As a nurse there, I mixed freely with the patients, and at the same time, despite the plain clothes, I was expected to maintain my status as a member of staff. The doctors, on the other hand, rarely mixed with the patients outside the therapeutic hours, and for this reason they collected about them auras of mystique and power. This perpetuated the whole dependency syndrome that partly led to the need for therapy in the first place.

A therapeutic patient is at one and the same time a victim of his history and the perpetrator of its continuing effect on

59

himself. The therapist must be prepared at one and the same time both to provide the necessary support needed by the patient whilst he makes the moves from falseness to authenticity and to avoid colluding with the patient in his dependency and infantile refusal to take responsibility for himself.

It is my belief that this delicate balance is more easily achieved if the therapist is *real*. This involves his being a *person*, rather than a mere role. The trouble with roles is that that they are not open and flowing, whereas life, and relationships between persons, are.

So the doctors at the 'Q' were not quite real, but shadowy figures that flitted the corridors, ministers of hope and unnameable powers. Outside sessions, patient behaviour was relayed to them by the nurses. Spies.

By contrast with almost all other mental institutions, the set-up at the 'Q' was imaginative, liberating and humane. Yet I did not regard it as being particularly successful. Partly this was because attitudes towards patients were full of ambiguity. On the one hand the staff purported to treat them like fully-fledged people, and on the other they were not allowed to forget that they were neurotic, patients, ill. As Szasz points out[1] being ill brings its own rewards in the form of diminished responsibility and care, and many of the patients clung to their state for this and other reasons. At the same time they were reminded of such things as their duty, their social responsibility, the importance of re-joining society on its own terms. There was present, subtly pervading the whole establishment, a polarity : on one hand, social health, on the other, social sickness. *What was missing was wellness in individual terms.* Another equivocal factor was the way in which an entire sub-community developed, leading to a tendency for members to become fixed within it according to the ways in which others saw them. Since becoming unneurotic involves breaking patterns and fixed modes of conduct, the tyranny of the community field was an obstacle to cure. It was also seductive to people unsure of their own identity, giving them an unreal sense of security, so that by contrast the outside world was

[1] In *The Myth of Mental Illness.*

seen as highly threatening, a faceless complex in which one's fragile identity could easily become lost.

The principal of the hospital, K., was a truly brilliant man – his mind flashed like so many knives. But he basked in himself a bit.

I had a strong feeling he disliked me the whole time I was there. Not that he ever said so – besides, I did my job well. I remember that when I first met him, and he gave his usual speech, I made it obvious that I was not impressed.

That didn't help. Nor, I think, did the fact that I was popular with most of the patients. I wasn't really nursing, but just being myself – to the extent that I was then – and achieving results. How dare I? Also I was sure he disliked my tendency to run everything I was involved in. Once he said to someone there, who passed it on to me: 'Is that chap Barnett trying to take over the place?' What, me? A mere £9-a-week auxiliary nurse? Naturally I would have done given half a chance. If I am going to travel I like to drive. I can sit alongside too, at a pinch, but back seats are quite unbearable. I still get car-sick if I travel any distance in the rear.

The doctors' meetings were a shock. At least at first. Once I had demystified myself they became amusing, but before that I could not believe that people capable of pettiness and jealousy and pride could help others towards states of health. I suppose, in my dreams, with which I still identified closely, in my magical ordered perfect world, all psychotherapists were Buddhas or Bodhisattvas, pure enlightened beings, free of ill-grace and discord. Anything less was a betrayal of the patient, introducing impurity into the sanitation of example and guidance. But the problems of neurosis lie not in imperfections, *but in refusal to admit to them*, in unreality, in *avoidance*. Nothing can be done, no change can be achieved, as long as we deal in the marvellous, in hopes and dreams, in ideals. The starting point is what we are, the truth about ourselves. There are strains in our society that preach otherwise. We are told we should cultivate goodness, and a certain kind of sweet virtue, that we should try to be better than we are. Trying is a pointless activity. If I am afraid, say, or greedy, what do

I gain by trying not to be afraid or greedy? Does this rid me of my fear or my greed? At best it covers up, and where is the truth in that? But if I *see* that I am jealous, say, or violent, see its workings within me, then there is a chance of change. Change, in fact, may begin at once.

As soon as I dropped my ideals and expectations of the doctors at the 'Q' I felt less critical of them as therapists and came to like some of them as people. In particular I developed a lot of affection for one. I'll call him Grant. Grant was the community doctor whilst I was there, and as such he was closely involved with nursing activity. He was a caring, sensitive man, very unassuming. Also he felt and showed gratitude, an appealing quality, particularly to me, for I seldom do. I take for granted, seeing what I do not get rather than what I get. Since I still have unfulfilled needs, I can never get enough, I always want more. When those ancient needs are fulfilled, or when I see that they will never be, cannot be, then probably I shall become aware of what is given to me, rather than what is missing, or withheld.

But like the other doctors Grant had some trouble with his role. At community meetings he could not let it go for a moment. It was as if he were defending the rank of the entire profession. As a result he would hide many of his rich personal qualities. In such ways do roles devour us. We hide ourselves to uphold them. Nationalism, party allegiance, religious fanaticism, sex chauvinism, professional fealty, all these are variations of the same disease : living by set answers rather than through spontaneity; identification with an abstraction at the expense of personal experience; the disease of self-sacrifice to an *idea*. And where does the idea come from? Usually it is put into our heads by those who wish us to sacrifice ourselves for *them*, and their constructions :

'They believe they are dying for the Class, they die for the Party boys. They believe they are dying for the Fatherland, they die for the Industrialists. They believe they are dying for the freedom of the Person, they die for the Freedom of the dividends. They believe they are dying for the Proletariat, they die for its Bureaucracy. They believe they are dying by orders of a State, they die for the money which holds the State. They believe they are dying for a nation, they die for the bandits that gag it. They believe – but why should one believe in such darkness? Believe – die? – when it is a matter of learning to live?"[2]

Believe – die. If I live for what I believe in I die to myself. Machines, gods, ideals, abstractions : first we invent them, then we become their slaves.

At the 'Q' my relationship with the Matron began to deteriorate. She liked to keep tight control on her staff, on everything. She was a tight person, physically, and it seemed that is how she wanted her world to be. Régimes, however liberal, are very difficult for me. I like to feel flexible and free. Fortunately I was soon helped in my rebellion by my new job as Entertainments Nurse. This was a highly roving commission, and the Matron's attempts to pin me down became quaint, since they clashed with my function. Also Grant saw I needed lots of room and was prepared to give me it, and trust me. Matrons are rarely like that, and this one wasn't. But then, matrons have many pressures upon them to fit neatly into schemes of things. Like most of us they are asked, frequently, to be not themselves but machines. Wheels within wheels. Systemized fodder.

Nevertheless I enjoyed being there – for a while. I can distance myself from my nature easily enough for a spell, I can play games; but then I get tired.

At the 'Q' I, a neurotic, played at nursing neurotics. This similitude enabled me to relate to them without judgement. At the same time it was slightly comic having a status that, no matter what I did, flapped over me like a flag. I was a nurse, and that fact conferred upon me a mode of relating and a power I could not escape.

Today, from my myth of mental health, I see neurotics differently. Like a judge, from my bench I look at them,

[2] Francois Perroux, *La Co-existence pacifique*. Quoted in Marcuse, *One-Dimensional Man*.

prisoners in the box. I peer at them through my imaginary truth-tinted glasses and perceive their living sins : their fear, their avoidance, their fatuous and spectacular games. With severity I shake my head, I reproach them, order them to put an end to their sad frolics. Sometimes I hear in me my mother, saying to me likewise, 'Stop this nonsense, Michael. Behave yourself.' Am I not then yet free of her?

But somewhere I do not judge myself, instead of others, so harshly. Instead I accept that I have a fetish about truth, that I am disposed to rip off masks, expose pretences, call bluffs. I batter at the doors of dungeons; I cannot let sleeping dogs lie. I insist that everyone be free and alive and real.

What is it to me, all this? As Sartre says : in choosing myself I choose all men, for I am how I want everyone to be. It is true too that it would make it easier for me to be whole and unafraid if others were too. For most of my life I was a king when among kings, a beggar when among beggars. I could be wise or foolish with the best and worst of them. Today my own level is more stable, but still I allow others to direct me; I use them to make my surrender.

But perhaps I am hiding something. Perhaps somewhere in me there is a white terror of happiness, love and fullness of being, a demon that insists that I do not deserve these things, and listening, I bow my head, and agree. So I fly from them the moment they are at hand. If I am possessed, somewhere, by a force negating life, and myself, how then can I allow others to remind me of this, since day in and out I live its contrary?

And so I devote my life to assaulting negation and distortion in others. I fight the vicarious fight, and avoid the real fight, the personal fight. No wonder I am a therapist.

Yet I lack interest in and care for the *details* of others' lives. I am concerned not with skirmishes, but with the major battle : life against death in life. I fight my war on all fronts. Others are both my allies and my enemies. I do not so much proselytize as recruit. My friends, my clients, my group members, myself – we line up against ourselves and we fight; we fight for life. Am I, after all, trapped myself by a belief, an ideal?

At the 'Q' it did not do to be too ill. They would talk about 'ego strength', and you had to squeeze out for them all you had of that. Letting go was a disaster. On the few occasions someone was injudicious enough, or desperate enough, to freak out, it was followed at once by panic meetings of various kinds : doctors, nurses and doctors, nurses and patients, patients, whilst everyone discussed the vital issue : could such disruption of the second-class peace that prevailed be allowed? Usually the answer was No. And so the patient, as a penalty for attempting to liberate himself, was thrust deeper into the system of psychiatric correction. This of course is in keeping with most political and psychological philosophies : the further you transgress set limits, the greater the forces brought to bear to press you back into formation.

To shout, to scream, to sob for a day, to face one's despair,[3] to believe that one's self is being stifled by society, or by one's family, these are seen as signs of sickness, whereas they could well be testimony of health.

I was detailed now and again to transport the ejected to deeper waters. These visits into the dark belly of psychiatry could be horrifying. Here was the medieval asylum little changed. There were no cells, no chains, but there were locked wards, nurses tough as gaolers, doctored minds, lost people on ECT and drugs looking bombed out of their right minds.

Long cold corridors, the jingle of keys, the sound of bolts being shot home, people lying about on beds whose only bearable reality was the stuff of dreams; all this would sicken me to my stomach. Most frightening of all was the sheer *immobility* of everything. It was all *there*, and yet its existence, as pervasive and powerful as the air we breathe, was only *apparent*. The system is everywhere unreal, yet it rules tyrannically the lives of free men.

Once it became impossible for me to complete my mission. My charge was a young undergraduate whose main fear was that his hair was falling out. He had, in his short stay at the 'Q',

[3] As Kierkegaard pointed out, the worst kind of despair is not to know you are in despair. See *The Sickness Unto Death.*

failed to co-operate with his therapist in his cure. That is to say, he had not yielded to treatment. His therapist had recommended him for transfer to a sterner establishment. When the young man saw and began to feel the chill and rigour of his new 'home', he began to sob. I too was close to tears. I had grown to know him quite well, and liked him. He had seemed troubled, but not excessively so. This was like being sent to Alcatraz for a parking offence. The sentence was itself the crime.

I rang the 'Q', spoke to the man's therapist, and said I could not leave him. It would feel like fratricide. He said I must. I replied I wouldn't. I said the patient refused to stay in any case. All the same he rang back and said in that case he would have to put the patient on a section, order compulsory detention. The receiving doctor took little interest. Either there was a package to deliver or there was not. I said there was not, and told the 'Q' therapist as much again. He said in that case he washed his hands of the whole matter. It was not possible for the patient to return to the 'Q'. If I would not leave him where I was then I would have to take responsibility for him myself, or get the boy's parents to do so and take him back home. I rang them. Reluctantly they came out, and they took him home.

As you see, St George and the Dragon. But then that story, like this one, has never been told from the dragon's point of view.

I left the 'Q' after six months there. This pleased some, upset others. I can remember how, after announcing my decision to my nursing colleagues, we all moved into our weekly seminar with K, the principal, and the Matron, and sat for two and a half hours, the eight of us, without uttering so much as one word. What power was at work to produce this, I do not know.

In any case, I left. I left because it was time, according to my tide. Or was it my cut-off point? During my last two weeks there, two major events occurred in my life: my mother died, and my son was born. For four days I stood alone, my mother gone, my son not yet here. But of course reality is not so clear cut. Mothers do not vanish so abruptly. They have been known often to ride on as far as their sons' or even their grandsons' graves.

What I left for, amongst other things, was the dole line. The die had been cast. I needed time to shuffle myself, start again even. Foolishly I believed it was writing I had to go back to. I took a cottage in Cornwall and wrote two books, both rewrites of old ones. This time they got closer to the printed page, but it was still a game; I was just playing it better.

In the meantime I had begun to have therapy. Laing had recommended to me P., a man younger than me, but well liked and much respected. Nevertheless I never felt happy with him. True, Laing had said I should get back to him in that case, but how could I? Since I was neurotic, how could I trust my own judgement? I continued, sharing nothing. Through him though I began at last to distinguish life from thinking. At that time I was submerging myself in Kierke-gaard, Sartre, Nietzsche, and Heidegger, believing that all I had to do was to find the right mix of them in order to solve, at the very least, all my own problems, not to mention those of the world. P., in his quiet, undirective way, showed me, or rather helped me to see for myself, that my thoughts were totally disconnected from my life, from reality. And through his incorruptible silence I found myself now and again on the brink of the void, dizzy at its vast absence. There, my feelings should have been. A Dionysus in me was tied to a stake, and though P., an Apollonian, might show me this was so, I did not believe he could help me to flow into that yawning space, and fill it with my caterwauling feelings, my anger, hate, grief, murderousness, laughter, desire and joy. P. would speak of facing one's own nothingness. Eventually, perhaps. But there was no bypassing this emotional gang.

No sooner did I move into Encounter groups than my trapped feelings starting flowing at once. Slowly they began to e-mote, and as they did, my energy began again to course around my body, so that my body awoke, insisting on its life, on self-expression, on its rightful place. What a world. Here if I felt anger I could express it, was in fact encouraged to do so. Here I could weep, leap, fight, attack, verbally rip to shreds. I could try, it seemed, *anything*, the only criterion being its authenticity to me, rather than its acceptability to others. What a way to discover myself, find out what it was that I was suppressing, inhibiting, disinheriting, so that *I* could decide what amongst these hoards of goods I wanted to incorporate into my outer life, and what I was going to keep secret, but know, if anything. I began to be reborn.

By contrast, just after this time, in a psychotherapeutic group I was attending twice a week, I was told by L., one of the therapists, after I had let rip with a lot of hostility against a fellow member, that if I wanted to be a therapist I would have to learn to control myself better than that. Imagine that. Roles first. Duty, control, pretence, self-abnegation – these were the criteria of therapeutic respectability.

Here lies the difference. Most psychotherapy, labouring under the dead body of Freud, accepts social reality as it is, and sees therapy as a method of helping the individual come to terms with its demands, and at the same time with the primitive and socially unacceptable needs of instinctive man. This plan, and the subsequent therapeutic strategy, is contained in the fundamental Freudian analysis of the human being, or his mind, into an ego, a super-ego, and an id. Roughly, the ego is the armed forces, the super-ego is the generals and the State, the id is the enemy – to be conquered, subdued and kept in chains. Central to this strategy is repression. Quite apart from the questionable nature of the quelling action, repression *never works*. The yoked forces have their say, often in unpredictable and devastating ways, like madness, epilepsy, emptiness, anguish, disease and death. Do not doubt that every cancer is an ultimate action of these repressed forces, a final triumphant laughing action of revenge. The Encounter approach is entirely different. It begins with the assumption that we are whole and that we can do nothing whilst at peace with ourselves until we at least know who and what we are, and *own* it. I have to own my anger, violence, envy, greed, cruelty, or else my life is going to be devoted to keeping those aspects of myself at bay, like armed creditors. The Human Potential movement sees that we have sacrificed ourselves *unknowingly*, as children, in the name of society, or of our parents. Let us then provide settings, experimental crucibles, says this movement, where we can express these parts of ourselves we keep muffled up and in chains; perhaps we can, after all, allow them life. And what we discover when we do this is – which was obvious all along – that none of these things, once they are allowed to flow, are *things* at all; they are not substantives : hate, anger, fear; but *processes*; and flowing, they give way to something else, often contrasting, like love or joy, or the sheer delight of being, as a person, on the move, as the emotions dammed up in the body, blocking the flow of energy, crippling, racking, begin to stream out, to e-mote. We also discover that our fears about the destructive nature of our repressed selves were highly fanciful, and that the reality is much less fearsome than the imagined. And finally we begin to make our own minds up about ourselves – in so far as this is possible, instead of going on accepting a package deal about the situation of being ourselves, as handed down through the generations. In short, we have a chance, in our mature years, to begin again, and this time to grow into ourselves, into our own process of continual becoming, through the stream of our own experience, and not through that of others, nor through the reifications of the thoughts and beliefs and poppycocking ideals of 'the silt and lees of bygone men'.

For this to happen we have to get back to the instruments of flow that we have lost – our emotions and our body. Both these flow naturally, that is to say, flowing is part of their nature. Not so the mind, which can repeat itself indefinitely like a stuck gramophone record, re-run the same circuit countless times, mill through the same maze incessantly, without finding an outlet. In our minds we can get stuck forever.

Freud was well aware of this pre-eminence of feelings :

'We remain on the surface so long as we treat only of memories and ideas. The only valuable things in psychic life are, rather, the emotions. All psychic forces are significant only through their aptitude to arouse emotions.'[4]

The body, too, is vital to our sense of reality, and to our flow. A live body is beautiful – though often enough so-called (aesthetically) beautiful bodies are not alive. A live body, fat, thin, long, short, this shape or that, is beautiful always, for a live body is an energized body, and energy is what we are. I respond to energy with my own energy. To emotions with emotions. To body with body. To mind with mind. But without our bodies we are not part of this world of energy, but zombies, living dead.

'Energy is the only life, and is from the Body . . . Energy is Eternal Delight.[5]

[4] From *Delusion and Dream and Other Essays*.
[5] *William Blake*.

Shell

For a year after leaving the 'Q' Hospital, psychiatrically I did nothing. My head was another matter. There, so much was happening it was something of a total mental institution in itself.

I stopped seeing P., but then, feeling close to the rapids, went back. He might not save me, but at least he might keep me afloat.

Writing feverishly, I discovered I could not lose myself by becoming a writer, or anything else come to that. And so I was left with myself still on my hands.

For six months I did nothing. The period from September 1968 until March 1969 is, in my memory, pale and bare, a blank wall. Naturally I did not do *nothing*. I had not yet learnt that fine art. I did far less, by keeping myself uselessly busy.

Then I took a job as a messenger boy. My duties consisted of hoiking parcels of plans between George Street and Brooks Mews in Mayfair. My beat was short, about a furlong, but I discovered many routes. I liked best the one that took me through the soft little oasis in Hanover Square. I liked to see the city people lying around in it, high on the flowers and the green and the fresh air. It was a lovely spring that year. I got to know that quarter of London intimately. As I staggered over and over again through my surroundings, they became not less but more substantial and real. I never reached the point of taking them for granted.

I felt about right, doing this job. It was strangely satisfying. My past of degrees, money, status, travel and words seemed to amount to nothing. Just games I had played. As a messenger boy I was at rock bottom, but at least I had my feet on the ground. I felt no humiliation. Nor, for once, was it difficult to take orders. The head of the post-room was a slim cockney, a cross between Andy Capp and Lupino Lane. I followed his instructions. I learnt from him how to roll a decent fag, and something of how to be independent and keep one's dignity, whilst still doing a proper job.

What is more I fell in love, for the first time in sixteen years (Pamela, my wife, was a special case). That was worth more than the fattest income, the supreme status. The woman in question, T., was the wife of a doctor, working with the company as a temporary typist. We arrived to begin work there on the same day, at the same time. I looked at her and said at once, 'Let's meet for lunch'.

We did, and every day after that. We used to go to a pub and I would get lovely stoned on her and the beer, so that the afternoons would swim by in a dream. I never noticed them at all sometimes. It was as if I had another working for me. T. was tall with bright, wide eyes that swam and sparkled and an excited face that made me drunk. She was the only woman I have ever met who could take a pee quicker than me. She used to beat me every time in the pub. Also she rolled her own cigarettes and smoked them in a rare way that would make my hair stand on end. We used to turn each other on the instant we met. Often, the entire time I was with her I would feel on the brink of exploding, without being in any danger of doing so. It was like a continuous living *coitus reservatus*. Once we took LSD together. It was a magic carpet ride, both instantaneous and endless. For the first time in my life I let go, for I felt at last that I had no need to prove anything, pretend anything, do anything, to be accepted and loved. I felt justified simply by being alive.

But it ruined everything. Bliss was there, for us to reach together, but neither of us could wait, nor did we have the time. T. was as hooked on her husband as I was then on my wife. Loving each other, having shared paradise together, we parted, preferring nothing to the repeated reminder of its absence and loss.

Then in May I found myself back in psychiatry. One morn-

ing, in the *Guardian*, I read of a new group with the pic-
turesque name of Campaign Against Psychiatric Atrocities, or
CAPA, that had been demonstrating outside a hospital against
the use of neuro-surgery there. It touched my own latent fury.
I rang the organizer, Peter Stumbke. He came to see me. He
felt I could be useful to him so we started working together
at once. Soon we were hand in glove, almost. Peter seemed
highly controlled and I could not see into his eyes – until he
smiled, when his entire face lit up and opened. Then, once
again, he would be inscrutable to me. Still, I found working
with him possible enough, and I began very much enjoying
the activity and the commitment. It was a relief from my
introspection and my blocked hatred for the mechanics of
psychiatry. CAPA demonstrated further, and I marched with
the rest, bearing my banner, 'Psychiatry Kills', but dissociating
myself from the hand that held it, like the woman in Sartre's
Being and Nothingness, who leaves her hand in that of the
man who wants her but refuses to notice that it is there. Like
her I was in bad faith. But I assured myself that the cause was
good, oh yes. I was demonstrating against a technique that
robbed men and women of any chance of wholeness – in this
life. And also against the working over of others in order to
avoid looking at the limitations of oneself. In a way, though
less perniciously, I was doing the same by demonstrating. What
I was demonstrating against, in gargantuan form, was part of
myself.

And against neuro-surgery – that last resort of the defeated
psychiatrist who, unable in his own terms to cure madness,
annihilates, removes the offending object, the recalcitrant
patient, from sight, thereby freeing himself to continue the
patterns of action he has embraced. If a mind offends thee,
pluck it out.

Experience is not a factor in the neuro-surgical equation. Nor
in that of chemotherapy. 'We are all chemistry anyway,' said
a chemotherapist to me in justification. I asked him for a test
tube of my experience. Also, what is the known chemistry of
love and grief, of anger and despair? What is the chemistry of
the heart that knows of these things, that knows too, if open,

of the ways to cure? What is the chemistry of intuition? Can it be injected? And if so, can my intuition be injected into you?

A chemotherapist discovers a common urinary constituent, or faulty potassium metabolism, amongst schizophrenics. He therefore argues, deal with this and we shall cure. How *naïf*! These are mere manifestations, physical statements of organic experiential realities. It is like trying to change a man's life by correcting his essays. To help a person change we have to get at nothing less than the fundamental ways in which he sees the world.[1]

Man, in a sense, is the geology of his own experience. That geology is governed greatly by infantile patterns of logic that have imposed themselves with such implacable power upon the organism as to become a virtual tyranny. For instance a young child might 'argue': my mother dislikes me; my mother is the whole world; therefore the whole world is against me. Enter the paranoiac. Or: my mother does not like me as I am. She would rather I were that than this. So I shall hide away this, and become that. Herewith the schizophrenic. To believe that drugs can change deep-seated patterns of thought like that seems to me to involve a monumental credulity.

Drugs, whether sedating or hallucinogen, can take us, and leave us, nowhere. The first can temporarily alleviate the pain of being what one is, and the second can sometimes show us what we are and can be. But drugged, we are not ourselves. We have been whisked away. In my experiences under drugs, I cannot be separated from them. It is *the drug and I* that are having the experience. Perhaps I can match it on my own, but before that I must travel the distance to it, so that when I am there I can remain, since I reached there unaided, without a crutch.[2]

[1] Groddeck, in *The Book of the It*, says something similar: 'Disease as an entity does not exist, except inasmuch as it is an expression of a man's total personality, his It, expressing itself through him. Disease is a form of self-expression.'

[2] Gurdjieff said: 'I can lift you to Heaven in a moment but you may fall back as quickly as you went up. If water does not reach 100 degrees [Centigrade] it is not boiling'. See T. de Hartmann, *Our Life with Mr. Gurdjieff.*

Beyond the wastes of drugs and ECT lies the guillotine of surgical leucotomy. This hideous practice consists of an incision or a cutting into the frontal lobes of the brain. The most harrowing aspect of it is its irreversibility.

Like ECT, it has an interesting history. Patients who had suffered brain injury involving damage to the frontal lobes became, it was noticed, more cheerful and free of worry. Therefore, it was argued, if similar damage was *deliberately* inflicted on depressives and schizophrenics then, hey presto! they might become transformed into cheerful happy-go-lucky souls. As you can see the sophisticated form of reasoning here matches the infantile patterns at work in the patients themselves.

Some patients died, others became epileptic, and others turned into cabbages. Hays, on the whole a sympathizer, writes :

'The results reflected these serious flaws : too many patients became totally inert and unresponsive; some died at once; others died some months later from obscure disturbances of control function exerted by the cortical areas involved; some patients improved but many did not, and a few became worse.

'Opposition to the operation, already strong, became stronger, but the surgeons and the psychiatrists who collaborated with them carried on. In 1950 the operation was banned in the U.S.S.R. . . .'[3]

But not in the UK, nor the USA. There the pioneers pressed on with their experiments, undeterred, if shaken, by the losses, and by the fact that comparative 'successes' seemed to lose all drive and spontaneity. There were many other impairments :

'An increased complacency and self-satisfaction with diminished interest in, or awareness of the feelings of others, can be one effect. Tactless and inconsiderate behaviour, usually the result of an attitude which is self-centred rather than deliberately offensive, are not uncommon. Together with the relief

[3] P. Hays, *New Horizons in Psychiatry.*

75

from acute self-criticism or despair there may be a corresponding loss in imagination, sensitivity, and intuition, so that judgement suffers, and while day-to-day intellectual capacity remains unimpaired, the fullest and highest ranges of mental life may no longer be scaled.

'Professor Golla has said that the basic change is an impairment in the power of ethical judgement; the patient's conscience, his views about right and wrong in both abstract and concrete situations, tend to become conventional rather than personally important. Sincerity takes second place to expedience.'[4]

I remember Susan from Adelaide, who came to see us through PNP. She had been leucotomized there. The doctors were excited, she said, about the new method. She was around, uncured, so they experimented on her. She had been eighteen at the time. She was now thirty. For twelve years nothing had interested her. Nothing reached her, she felt nothing. Her voice was as thin as a hair. She was working as a secretary – to a consultant psychiatrist in a mental hospital. Was she hoping to regain her lost part?

ECT hinders psychotherapy. Leucotomy renders it impotent. Here is how John Rosen, the imaginative creator and practitioner of Direct Analysis, sees them in his experience :

A number of attempts were made to treat patients psychologically who had received psychosurgery and to date I find these patients absolutely hopeless. I've thought here, if they cut these patients' heads off altogether, then surely the psychosis would be cured.'[5]

Rosen also found a direct correlation between successful outcome through his methods and the *absence* of shock treatment in the patient's psychiatric history. At that time, in the late forties and early fifties, many of his patients came to him with a history of more than 100 shock treatments, and in one case,

[4] D. Stafford-Clark, *Psychiatry Today*.
[5] J. N. Rosen, *Direct Analysis*.

a young girl of sixteen, more than 400 applications of ECT
or insulin shock therapy! Consider the mentality of such per-
sistence. Rats are more intelligent. If they fail often enough,
they search for alternatives.

Since the mid-fifties the method has at last fallen out of
fashion. I use this word consideredly, though I am referring
to acts against people. But today a few practitioners still continue to employ it, with some conviction. One eminent surgeon,
B., was doing so in 1969, and it was largely against him and
his methods that CAPA had been demonstrating, when
reported about in the *Guardian*.

I remembered B. from a television documentary I had seen
some time before. He had been shown at work and I had not
been impressed. In fact his methods frightened me, for they
were so clinical and overbearing. He knew best – an attitude
that is not uncommon amongst the medical fraternity,[6] on
matters I personally consider to be far outside their incontest-
able jurisdiction. B. even produced a leucotomized patient who
dizzily admitted his gratitude for being robbed of part of his
brain!

But many things about CAPA bothered me. There was,
for example, my fellow demonstrators. They wouldn't talk to
me, polite greetings and exchanges apart, and when finally
two did, over lunch, they seemed to know nothing of the issues.
One told me he was demonstrating because he was tired of
paying so much income tax. Without psychiatric institutions
this could come down. The other said she knew very little
about the Movement or what it stood for, but she had been
asked to come by friends, and so she had. Peter too
seemed to me oddly uninformed about the state of psychiatric
play for someone leading an antipsychiatric militant group. He
appeared to know little about Szasz and Cooper and Laing.

Although he gave me quite a lot to do, and some say in
matters, Peter would often point out, rightly enough, that he
was CAPA's creator, and would make all major decisions.
But there seemed to be more to it than that. Often we would

---

[6] Reflecting the crippling and oppressive hierachy prevalent today
in both the social and the individual organism.

agree on something, then he would ring me the next day with his mind changed, brooking no argument. Several times we agreed to change the movement's grisly name, would find a new one, be happy with it, and then would come the call to say it was to stay as it was.

CAPA's mission was to topple institutional psychiatry. Part of the campaign was the methodical collection of evidence of psychiatric outrage; in the hope, I wondered, that in the event the general public, horrified, would clamour for the dismissal or the outlawing of the entire psychiatric profession, *in toto*? Or else perhaps, so confronted, these guilt-ridden gentlemen would resign, in a single body, from shame!

But what was to take its place, I wanted to know? Being on the brink of madness I needed something to be there, to take care of me. I needed an alternative, not a holocaust.

Disagreements grew, and yet I hung on. CAPA was *there*, and, like a business house, it was providing me with work, with something to do. Like millions, I compromised in order to fulfil my needs, drawing a veil where I cared not to look.

Even when the crunch came I held on grimly, whilst abjuring and impeaching without mercy. This happened the evening Sidney Briskin came round to Peter's. He, along with Laing and others, had set up Kingsley Hall, that psychic community in the East End that was an experiment in 'letting be' rather than 'fixing'. I think Sidney came because he was the sort of person who liked to know what was going on. I liked his energetic hair and his large, live face; both seemed fully grown whereas I felt callow, a mere stripling. Now I respond to the full, the large, and the mature, with delight rather than longing or admiration.

Sidney sat there under my gaze and said, 'I hear CAPA is connected with Scientology.' I replied at once, brisk and business-like: 'Nonsense, no connection at all.' I became aware I was speaking alone; I had expected a chorus. I shot a look at Peter. He was still, his face impassive and smooth. But at once I sensed disquiet. Briskin went on, a gentle executioner, 'I understand you at least have been a Scientologist for a number of years.' I was shattered to hear Peter confirm this.

He went on, saying that CAPA was separate, a personal affair, but already I was lying numb amongst ruins. I heard Sidney, far off, remarking on the coincidence that Scientology was currently mounting a mammoth campaign against psychiatry. I heard Peter repeating, 'CAPA is separate. CAPA is separate'. But I had gone. I was still there, inserted, but I had withdrawn my serum.

Working against one personal enemy, I had nourished another. Fighting for a cause, rather than for myself and my beliefs, I had allowed myself to be a cat's paw. So, I had been exposed for the blind vector of energy that I was : exploitable, manipulable, a willing innocent. Or cunning enough to avoid seeing, to the point of blindness, what would cut me off from fulfilling my immediate needs. How many times I had done that in my life, with women !

Looking back over my month or so with CAPA I saw that my gullibility and blindness had been prodigious. Mentions of East Grinstead, the Scientology country centre, the innocence of my fellow-demonstrators, the perfection of the banners, Peter's evasions, the obedience of the rank and file, the general absence of psychiatric awareness, of idealists, of committed people; I had ignored *everything* in order to continue. I could not blame Peter. It was I, chiefly, who had deceived myself.

After Sidney went I challenged Peter, wearily. He apologized, said he had not revealed his own involvement with Scientology, guessing I had the usual prejudice against it. At this point I somersaulted. Had I? After all, all I had to go on was a negative response to some soggy pages written by Ron Hubbard, the movement's founder, some press reports, to which surely I would give no credence, and a handful of scientologists I had met and not personally trusted. But then, they had left. I felt myself weaken, as need and justice took a hand. I asked Peter to enlighten me.

He praised, then handed me a few copies of their magazine. They were anti-psychiatry issues. I was repelled by them. I said I was finished, and left.

Yet still I could not quite make the break. An old pattern.

When my whole being reacted against something, still I would hold on by the skin of my teeth. I had to leave home again, this time my wife, before I cured myself of this terror of letting go, once and for all. Next morning I rang Peter, hoping, to my own disgust, to find a way of re-fusing, soldering the break. But Peter had grown cautious. Now that the cat was out of the bag I would be more wary. I suppose he guessed I would fight inch by inch. He said he thought it best we should part. But he wasn't sure. We agreed to meet later that day. In the meantime I talked the matter over with David Eddy. He said it was clear I could not go on, feeling as I did. I saw my own deceits, my need to reach the conclusion that I should continue, at almost all costs; my fear of standing alone. When I met Peter I told him it was all over. He agreed, maintaining he was unhappy about me, and my 'new left' influence on the movement, as he called it, which was distracting it from its original goals.

This schism at the core of this rollicking movement of a handful of people, or really of only two, effectively, Peter and me, already written up by the *Guardian* and the *Daily Mirror*, now reached the dignified columns of *The Times* :

'A difference of opinion has arisen among the militant opponents of modern psychiatry. Since March a group calling themselves the Campaign Against Psychiatric Atrocities have demonstrated in Harley Street four or five times, waving placards with slogans such as "Psychiatry Kills" and "Psychiatry Does You In". Now Mr Mike Barnett, who was for a time the campaign's acting secretary, has left to organize a new movement – "not a protest, but a positive alternative . . .".'

'Stumbke says his parting with Barnett was amicable – "a difference over methods not aims" – but Barnett seems to have been also concerned at the backing the campaign was receiving from the scientologists (whose enmity towards psychiatry has been manifested in recent publications). Stumbke, however, denies that his campaign has any links with scientology.'[7]

After leaving Peter I returned home. There I sat awhile,

[7] *The Times*, August 11, 1969.

pounding with energy, my field removed, a webless spider. I had to do something, I had to go on.

I turned to myself, for once. Why the need to hitch myself to another, to something existent? Could I not create from scratch? Why did I persuade myself so often that I lacked the strength? Because my mother had told me so often I was not very strong? Was she ruling me still, that lovely insidious phantom? The time had come to toddle, to take my first steps alone.

I wrote a short article. It came out through my pen, catching me unawares, like a snake in the tailored grass, a creature of myself and my milieu – charged then like storm air with the dazzling reversals of Marcuse, Laing and Cooper: the mad, the neurotics, the outcasts and the outsiders – these were the truly sane ones, the forces of change, the negators of the negation, the forerunners of the new man. Naturally I was a member of this vanguard. I was neurotic, nearly mad, an outsider, and almost unemployable into the bargain. As with many at that time, excitement at this headstand in values overlaid my emptiness and despair.

Nevertheless it is those with an inner discontent, often, who build social alternatives, or move for radical change. Aware of their own faults, they spy those in society. Whereas the smug, the complacent, the comfortable – like as not they accept their social situation lock, stock and barrel. They become ballast of the *status quo*.

Gurdjieff called inner struggles *friction*, and maintained that without it there could be no inner unity; without it a man would not change but remain such as he is. But there could be good friction and bad friction – the latter leading nowhere.

The dissatisfied may move from inner upheaval outwards belligerently against 'the system' – that nebulous abstraction that is nothing but people – in such a way that the individuals who compose it are seen and treated by the activist just as impersonally as they are by the purveyors of the system. Others in discontent will move towards other persons, with whom to do things differently, try new life-styles.

F

The article offered this, laced though with a political onslaught, a neurotic transvaluation of values, and revolutionary glory. Always an individualist, that is to say, always unable to let go of myself, and love, I had developed, to compensate, messianic qualities. From the beginning I had opposed them remorselessly, even when the role of leader had been thrust upon me, doing all I could to avoid the confirmation of what was, at one and the same time, one of my deepest wishes and one of my greatest fears. At the time of that article I was still in the throes of conflict about this aspect of myself. Consequently, then, and almost throughout my time with PNP, I was both thrusting myself forward and holding back, refusing any cloak of authority proffered me.

Here is the article, published by *IT*, the underground journal, in July 1969, in issue 59 along with an interview with R. D. Laing, another with Mick Jagger, a review of *Bayou Country*, Creedence Clearwater Revival's latest record, The Adventures of Jerry Cornelius in cartoon by Mal Dean and Michael Moorcock – illustrious company :

THE SICK SCENE

'Psychiatry is politics. The whole scene is under the thumbs of the greys. Pretty well everywhere today the dead men, the square men and the greys are running things, calling the tune.

'But inside some people colour and love and soul won't just lie down and die. Inside they are at war – true selves fighting grey goblins implanted from outside. Some of these people, these heroes of the resistance, are commonly referred to as mad.

'Many are put away. Where they suffer humiliation, degradation, manipulation, contempt, derision. Where they undergo electro-shock, massive tranquillization, straitjacketing and insulin comas. And all in the bright names of succour and science.

'What does this surgery of souls achieve?

'For the State, success means a new obedience and conformity, more socio-economic units; failure means it has someone labelled chronically insane to take care of for life.

'But for the so-called patient, the State's failure is his failure, and the State's success is his failure too. In other words he can't win. He doesn't stand a chance. He is doomed.

'And they say 1 in 8 of us has that fate in store.

'Grim. Grim but real, and there's precious little light on the horizon. In fact, judging from current enthusiasm for empiricism and expediency things will probably get worse. And worse.

'Unless. And that's what PNP (People for a New Psychiatry) is all about : Unless.

'We see the mental hospital as largely an anachronism. And current modes of treatment in all but a very few as medieval and barbaric. The same goes for psychiatric wings. We think the lot should be scrapped. We would like to see State finance provided for the right people to set up sanctuaries in which those in great conflict and distress as a result of what has happened to them, what has been done to them, can take their inner trips, find themselves, work through their living experience in an open environment offering care, understanding and concern. We don't see this as the one answer, or even as necessarily the best answer, but compared with the present ugly scene it's utopian and would do for a start.

'That's the hope for the State scene. What about us, the individuals? PNP are forming a network of people who are willing to help transform psychiatry in its thought and deed, help each other, help others who need help, not by DOING things to them, but by opening themselves to them, offering care, perhaps a little understanding, and concern. A programme not of interference but of extended liberty, not of manipulation but of nurture and growth.

'Psychiatry is politics. And the blatant aim of current politics is to keep things more or less as they are. That means stifling all the forces of change. People who break down because they cannot find a way to live sanely in an insane society are shattered forces of change. Kept whole and mended, restored to themselves, they might threaten. So whilst they are broken and defenceless the lackeys of the power system step in and make new men and women of them. New docile noddy people, new but no longer themselves. But State slaves. If people still believed in the soul this would be described as murder. As it is it is called treatment. It is even called humane.

'Intelligent and well-meaning people defend this humanless tinkering, this human masonry, this working in stone. They point to the "cures", to the alleviation of suffering, to the thousands of grateful patients who can no longer remember what was wrong. They have become normal, they can function, they have lost their anxiety. But what was wrong was what they are and what they have also lost is themselves.

'The Good label the rest Bad. The Sane label the rest Mad. The sane make war, slaughter each other by the million, lock people up for years, for life. The mad take trips, talk strangely, act oddly, but they rarely kill each other and they don't imprison and oppress. So are they really mad? Are the others really sane?

In other words, Who's Got The Sanity?

'Anyone wanting to join in changing the scene, a revolution no less, contact :

Mike Barnett,
Operations Room for PNP.'

What a manifesto! What terror! Where had it come from? Was I, after all, talking about my mother? Was it her spectre I was fighting against, her attempts to make me in her own image? Was it my terror of her, her power, her monolithic presence, that I was transferring on to psychiatry?[8] Was my fight against my own fear of walking away from her, and finding my own centre, my own strength?

And was PNP, this bawling infant, my attempt to give birth to and rear for myself a mother who would provide and care without threatening, through control, my separate reality? What is more, as creator, it was I who would be in charge. Was my paranoia then merely the continuing expression of my infantile and childish terror of a subtly manipulative mother?

It is possible. And yet I could only transfer that primitive

[8] A power and a presence I of course gave this fine, heroic lady.

fear and impotence to psychiatry to the extent that it resembled part of my image of her in its approach to its children – the patients.

Psychiatry reflects the nuclear family, its control system, its vesting of total authority in parents, as psychiatry vests it in the psychiatrist.

The psychiatrist, in our society, will continue to see himself as above suspicion, and beyond challenge from the patient, as long as parents regard themselves in the same way vis-à-vis their children.

Without extravagance, without moonshine, I *know* I have as much to learn from Shem, my five-year-old son, as he has from me, and I am glad to the extent that I allow this to happen.

When will we allow ourselves to be brought up by our children?[9] When will the psychiatrist learn from his patients, the lion-tamer from his lions, the West from the East? When will it be the leper's turn to kiss the saint?[10]

In the meantime, PNP was launched.

[9] For a brilliant and cogent argument against the tyranny of the family, see David Cooper's *Death of the Family*.

[10] See the end of Laing's essay 'Us and Them', in *The Politics of Experience*.

Dune

I felt like the original ice-cream man. I had rung a bell to an avalanche. The phone rarely stopped ringing, many arrived unheralded at the door, mail poured in, and under the deluge I bloomed. I was in my element. I was involved socially and inter-personally, *on my own terms*.

For weeks I saw a stream of people, one at a time, always one at a time. Partly this was a way of keeping control. Everybody knew what was happening according to *my* account. But I am unjust. I was also *serious* about what was being created, and I wanted to get to the essence of those to be involved *at once*. In a sense there was an element of interviewing in these meetings, but at least I allowed myself to be interviewed likewise.

Through action I began to understand what I was up to. Apparently I was trying to set up a lay network of *persons*, not therapists, not psychiatrists, who would be available to relate to others, patients or potential patients, as *themselves*. I was seeking others (I did not question *my own* aptness for a moment) who, in doing this, would enrich the downcast and the needy, the blocked, the frightened and the low, and move them towards their own growth and flow. I was looking, in short, for *nourishers*, preferably with thaumaturgic gifts.

At the same time as I was assuring everybody that PNP would have no laminations, that all were helpers and helped, either at different times or simultaneously, I did not believe it. An organized hierarchy is one thing, natural differences, at a point of time, in awareness, freedom, and depth and strength of neurosis are another. I was opposed to the political people who *on principle* would not permit a sniff of difference between people to be overtly acknowledged, although, from guilt and uncertainty, I did allow myself to be deflected by them for a while.

Each day for three or four weeks I saw up to fifteen people who had responded, taking time, but making up my mind, in my usual fashion, quite quickly, as to the level each person would take in network operations. Mainly I had in mind two levels, though the second had subdivisions : I wanted a central group, an infrastructure, around which the rest would gather, like filings around poles. The filings themselves might then become magnetized, and add to the poles, but that would be if it came to be. In the meantime I wanted firm nuclei, substantial foundations. I was matching my own view of life as a way, a path taken to a goal which can only be reached, or be seen to have been reached, without seeking. To reach this goal, without trying, is difficult, largely because we have been distracted by a shower of useless objectives we have been enjoined to aim for, but which are empty and worthless. Just as others have diverted us from the simple aim of being ourselves, and reaching the natural state of flow of that, so we may need others to thrust us back on our path.

But apart from this attempt to stamp my own world on others and society, it became obvious later, when the rueful equalizers had their way, that some kind of central core was necessary for *survival*. Without it, the links loosen, the conglomerate force is lost, and the whole movement with its potential for growth and infection is in danger of being washed away by the tides of social patterns and conformity.

As far as I was concerned PNP was a movement against expertise, formalized power, the cult of knowledge, and the collected atrocities and idiocies of modern mechanistic psychiatry. It was an attempt to shake sick and critical states of mind and being out of the grip of psychiatry and its formalized patterns of approach that, apart from psychotherapy, reduced individuals to units, suitable cases for treatment; leaving them free to find their own level, via the setting of their own limits, in open interaction, where special persons, equipped not with theoretical knowledge but with awareness and insight, would be available to take part in the sick person's interaction in times of crisis, but as *persons*, as who and what they were, with no authority other than that, and no sanctions such as shock treatment or institutionalization to falsify the situation.

From the few hundred people I saw in the first weeks I picked fourteen. How? I cannot justify my methods of assessment, but those I picked, whatever they might have satisfied in me, had things like strength and space and life movement. It is also true that those fourteen chose me, but this is clouded by the fact that if they elected to join PNP then they automatically chose me. Of the others, many were in states of some desperation, made worse by their common rejection of psychiatry. PNP would find work, learning if an alternative to professional exploitation of the sick was possible. A large market was ready and to hand.

I wrote to the fourteen, suggesting we should all meet. I arranged a time. On the night all fourteen came. I was very excited at this. Time had elapsed, people cool and waver, I had hardly expected a full return.

Now that it was here Pam, my wife, joined too. Till then she had remained uncommitted. She was very impressed by the full turnout. She felt it meant well. Also it restored some faith she had lost in human nature. Perhaps too it gave her new faith in me.

It was a good meeting, because that is what we did – meet. Needing no pretensions, we could care or goon. The energy level was very high and, though none of the others had previously met, united. The opposition to psychiatry seemed formidable that night. Shem, then one and a half, sat up seriously throughout, proof positive that energy abounded. There was no doubt that we were launched.

Sixteen names, addresses and phone numbers on a sheet – that was PNP. The lists found their way all over London and beyond, and people began making contact. At times it became too much for those central, available, and popular, who had to call for reinforcements.

What were we offering? In a sense, nothing; not doctors,

we could not offer cure; as laymen we could not specifically offer anything. We were people, what we were, and we could be with. If that was any use to you, with her, with him, with me, then you were part of PNP.

Soon the name changed. We could not be for a *new* psychiatry. Where would that land us? We were for none at all. 'Leave them alone and they'll come home.' We were for people levelling with each other and finding out where that landed them in relation to each other. For people, then, *not* psychiatry.

We need experts because we do not trust ourselves. In fact every one of us excels every expert within ourselves. We give away our power, then bow down and obey. The greatest healing agent is love, assuredly. Where can that love be in a state psychiatry?

'Who would suspect,' writes J. N. Rosen, analyst, 'that man's humanity to man could be a medicine?'

What is more we were geared to allay fear – the ringmaster of every neurosis. If it is fear which keeps you where you are, fear must find out about itself, and this can only be done in an atmosphere of love and trust. I do not want to be misunderstood about this 'love'. I am far in thought here from peacenikking or lovie-doveying; by it I mean something like acceptance, which is nice wise love.

What happened? People visited people, explored, found out, moved on. This was therapeutic in any sense. There was much in common and many were glad to learn of each other, and then about each other. There was no credo, not even a clause. It was every man be himself. That's all. Many toured the whole network, sounding out, discovering themselves and others. It was a free tour for interpersonal experimentation. We became important to some, that member, this member, those members, and provided a link where one was wanting. Clearly our motives were not solely altruistic, as they never are. There was something in it for us, far beyond any sense of being a good boy. We too were experimenting; we too were frightened, if not for now, then for the future. The shadow of differentiation is cast by space and time. Have I space in my experiment for your experiment? If so, we shall consider yours. If not, then let us consider mine.

Here you might get anti-psychiatry, there, politics. There, playing with the children, there astrology, mysticism, or a kind of psychotherapy. There, tea and cakes and a wander through the park. You might well get a smoke too, to the sound of Crosby, Stills and Nash. Who knows what went on?

Of course a practitioner would wave aside such naïvety and parade his knowledge of the workings of man. But every theory is a *slant*, which their advocates forget. We have to give the mind the slip. Then we are in touch with the fullness and rightness of things. Generalizations are merely a shorthand. But then they bunch together and form a theory. Their original purpose is forgotten. The mind, the dealer in this new human value, theory, gains ascendance, and we are lost.

> Mind working is man
> Mind working fast is mad
> Mind working slow is saint
> Mind stopped is God.[1]

In Zen they talk of 'on being without a head'; the doctrine of no-mind, *wu-hsin*. We are taught, over here, to be far from this. So many of us lead with out head, and stay in it, wondering why we cannot capture the joy of experience, when our bodies are its seat, and our emotions are its expression, and we are so severed from both.[2]

A good ear can do wonders, one that can listen, that is. A good heart can work miracles. An open breast can coax into life. Love and acceptance can make an autumn bloom. A freedom to be and to let be can set free. In truth we can all work miracles with each other. How absurd are those desperate inventions, chemical drugs and ECT!

There we were, to be called on if you wanted.

You came because you wanted to see one of us, person to

[1] Meher Baba.
[2] Besides, what we 'know' is so influenced by what we 'do not know', that it cannot really be said that we know anything.

person. Sometimes you came because anybody would do; it was better than nobody, and, at the other end, most psychiatrists were, in the main sense, nobodies too.

Friends, if you have them, are seldom right for confession or experimentation. Their images of us are as a rule too fixed, their patterns jell with ours into a fixed relationship that repels and intimidates change. PNP was usefully between friend and professional, between therapist and nobody, between introspection and a false sociability. Here and there it hit a bull's-eye.

A young man came to me with a secret. It was trivial, he knew, and it was still burning him up. There was no one he could tell, to share its amazing existence. No friend would suit, he said, they would marvel, or make fun of him. He told the secret, which was light opera, but naturally linked to something far deeper in his experience, and then sat and sobbed – with relief. So, I had taken confession, not of sin but of shame. I cannot doubt the goodness of the flow of tears, nor of the body's relief as it let go its load.

We were confessor, witness, audience, therapist, laboratory, saviour (here and there), last straw, free coffee house, bun shop, social club, cupid, shelter, Mum and Dad, long-lost friend, Good Samaritan, first of the few. And all the time we were ourselves, but all these to others. Imagine a natural system of healing based on people being themselves to each other. Yes, but one can as easily imagine a toxic system based on the same footing. Because of this I do not doubt that, due to some of its aspects, psychiatry *can* save. Oddly psychiatry can save people from people, just as people can save people from psychiatry. *In a way* psychiatry is a machine designed to save people from people. (It is what it does to them *then* that is the problem.) This is a new perspective, that stands everything on its head. A complains about B. Actually it is A who is killing B. But A sees himself or herself as the victim. He calls in expert C. C agrees with A about the behaviour of B, and takes him off A's hands. *Thereby B gets free of A, and lives.* It is the performing bear saying, 'If that guy throws me any more of that honey, I'm going to get up and dance.'

Unfortunately C and his bases often are not much less murderous than A. Moreover when they are, it is usually C's aim to restore B to A, if and when he has healed from their last interaction together. Of course, this is what the British public schools did too. The poor little buggers didn't stand a chance.

There is no doubt we kept hundreds off the mental health farms. It was possible to see quickly the way in which some who came grew in their degree of self-trust. Trust thyself, say the Zen Buddhists. Then nothing else is required.

And be aware. Actually the two amount to the same thing, methinks. The more you become aware of yourself the more you know of yourself, and the more you see how you contain all the answers, and are to be infinitely trusted.

That is much of what the Humanistic Psychology movement is all about. Returning to one's self as the ground of all being. Changing value from society to humanity, from ought to be to can be, to what is. Let us see what *men* we can become, not citizens. When we meet as men, real men, we shall have our society. It shall be composed of the set of relationships between us.

PNP was a small society. But it was free, in the sense that restrictions were placed on it and in it by individuals. There were no 'lights out!', but I might say that I wanted to go to bed now. I wouldn't close down but I would tell my visitors that it was time to go.

Well and good, perhaps. But who is going to offer this kind of openness with their home and life and self? It is a tall order. Looking back I marvel at the time given by some of the members. For Pam and me for a long while it was almost continuous. Others too were devoting many hours each week to a sharing with others – whom they had not chosen. What were our motives? There was certainly more in it than meets the eye.

The Myth, the penultimate truth of experience, according to Hinduism,[3] is the slaying of the Dragon-Father. Perhaps each one of us was fighting this timeless fight by freeing our-

[3] See in particular Coomaraswamy, *Hinduism and Buddhism.*

92

selves (or others; at this depth of myth it amounts to the same thing) from the Father-Tyrant in his guise of psychiatry. Some of us, who had had truck with this psychiatry, believed we were fighting for a cause : the freedom of the patient. But, in truth, *we* were both psychiatrist and patient. The war is *always* a war with oneself, usually some shape of the struggle against our own dragon – that belongs to others, to our father, and, belching the fire that we stoke ourselves, paralyses us.

Nevertheless whatever our motives, or the level upon which we wish to view them, the time and space that small group of people offered to others enabled PNP to come into being.

In a way we were educators.[4] We saw the world often much in the same way as did those who came to see us, but yet we were coping. We were, in a sense, giving lessons in this, just as a psychotherapist does, except that he will usually offer, or even press, an entirely different perspective on his client, whereas we were offering, if you like, skills in being a dropout, or an outsider, or a rogue amongst the herd.

Later, as I intend to tell, the list became much more of a net of reciprocal relationships, just people connected to people. Well and good, probably. But it was never what I had in mind for PNP, as those instrumenting the change well knew and, I think, resented.

We need soil to grow, and soil for us is communication – with the environment, including other people. But not all persons are nourishing to us, some nourish nobody, but are toxic, at least for the time. The roots of plants stretch out towards nutrition. Often we are prevented from doing the same, surely a natural act, by pride, or a false understanding of the notion of equality. People are not equal to us; that is surely our experience. But we obliterate this in order to embrace a mere idea which, if it is true, is so on an absolute, rather than on an existential level.

Being ill is a choice of being. It is not a particularly reward-ing one, but it does, at some level, appear, or did once appear, to its subject, to have its merits, not least of which was sur-

---

[4] That psychiatry ought to give way to education is the view of the American psychiatrist, Thomas Szasz. For his books, see bibliography.

vival, and the assurance of the essentials of living, such as food, shelter, and perhaps love, or a token of it.

To choose differently, to make a fresh choice when the original choice[5] is experienced as unsatisfactory and wanting, requires a setting in which experiments can be made, can be dared to be made, and PNP was an attempt to provide such settings, just as Growth centres do (but these with a wide variety of techniques that lead participants towards the kinds of experiments in being that have proved bountiful for others).

The trouble with much of modern psychiatry is that it offers a mechanistic cure, like an elaborate iridescent aspirin. But to the patient undergoing the cure, existentially, nothing happens, and this is a vital flaw because people are not machines but existential beings who can change, or will change, only as a result of seeing the world and their relationship to it in a different way.

It is little use putting a person in a place from which the world may look different, with for example the use of drugs, if he cannot get there existentially under his own steam. To return there, or remain there, he becomes dependent on the external means, the drug. Apart from the artificiality of the achievement, drugs have a pervasive, not a local, effect upon the system, so that other drugs become necessary in order to offset side-effects. And so on *ad infinitum*. We end up in fact with what Gregory Bateson describes as 'a bag of tricks'.[6]

But on a different level the vital flaw in psychiatry is the fact that it offers, *from outside the person*, a cure at all.

For we can, in the event, only cure ourselves. The psychiatrist is chiefly useful through his demonstration to the patient that he, the psychiatrist, cannot cure the other, the patient, since he, the patient, is ill *from choice*. Only the patient can cure himself – through a decision to alter the choice he has

[5] Satre discusses 'original choice', which he compares with the psychoanalytical 'complex', in *Being and Nothingness*. Both, he says, are total, prior to logic, and decide the patient's attitude to all things. Compare Groddeck's 'It'.

[6] See his excellent essay, 'Conscious Purpose versus Nature', in *The Dialectics of Liberation*, (Ed. D. Cooper).

made to be ill. But before this can happen it is usually necessary, or at least helpful, if the patient realizes his own responsibility for his condition, and ceases to see it as something inflicted upon him from the outside, or by his 'unconscious'. If he is victim, he is also perpetrator. Who else could be?

Wherever we are, that is where we wish to be. We may *wish to wish* to be elsewhere, but that is only an image. We choose everything about ourselves at every moment. First we have to see that. If we do not, then we are at war with ourselves, and our energy is consumed by the conflict, so that nothing can happen, no change can take place. If we see that we *will* to be where we are, if we can then *be* there, then we can move, we can flow. Then change will take place, since change is intrinsic in all things. A Chinese emperor asked his Buddhist retainer to give him something that would provide caution when he was feeling high and hope when he was feeling low. The Buddhist gave him a talisman on which was written 'nothing lasts'. This is true, but unfortunately we do have the ability to arrest the natural flow of things. Neurosis does this, so does all hanging on to what we have or are, and all hanging on to what we are not, to concepts and ideals and hopes, which is united with a refusal to accept what we are, what is.

There is no way of *forcing* a person to alter the choice he is making. Sometimes he can be tricked into experiencing an alternative, and through this come to realize *wholly* the preferability of this alternative, so that he comes to adopt it and change. To outwit another in this way, to elude habitual and impoverished choices, requires considerable skill. Zen masters tend to have it. So do the best therapists and group leaders, and others everywhere.

Frequently this skill makes use of frustration. That is, the sick person or the seeker is constantly thrown back on himself in order that he should discover his own healer, his own fulfilment, within himself. This is what Perls describes as moving from environmental support to self-support. This is also in line with Eastern philosophy, which teaches that we are *all* Buddhas, or that we all have an *atman* that is an expression of *Brahman*, or It, or Everything, or whatever you like to call the source and expression of life itself.

The neurotic spends his life and energy living from his moon instead of his sun. Thus he lives a false existence, for he takes his moon for his sun. Or not exactly false, so much as ersatz and unreal. And much of his energy is taken up too in *avoiding* his own sun. For the life of the sun in him is powerful and full of feeling. The sun resides in the belly, the moon roosts in the head.[7] The latter is ordered and comparatively calm (except when disturbed by the activity of the entombed sun); the former is powerful and constantly active, flowing, affecting the whole organism. We flee from this into our heads and pretend we are living.

So long have we been estranged from our centre that we experience life from there, when we fight our way back, as often painful. So we flee again.

But this pain must be faced if we are to truly live. The true personal revolution is by way of the inner hell. The pain has to be experienced throughout one's body and being. It has to be allowed to *flow*. In doing so it will be replaced perhaps by another feeling, perhaps painful, perhaps pleasurable; if pleasurable, we cannot hang on to that either. It too must be allowed to flow, in response to what the ancient Chinese used to call the Tao, or the way of things. But the way of things is not out there, but in here, within, it is our flow in response to the world as we experience it.

Moreover there comes a point when, sometimes, pain turns into pleasure. Actually the sensation itself does not change; what changes is our *opinion* of it.

Blood and life flowing back into a numb hand is experienced as pain. But it is possible to welcome it as pleasure. That is not quite what I mean. We tend to regard whatever is new, even new and stronger life, as painful, because it appears to ask something of us in the way of effort, or change; it threatens

---

[7] Compare the *Tao Te Ching*: 'The sage is concerned with the belly and not with the eyes.' See also, in particular, K. Durkheim's, *Hara*. Hara is the Japanese word for belly, and this is unquestioned by the wise, according to Durkheim, as the primal centre of man.

our cosiness, our lunary existence. But of course it asks nothing, except that we be, not what we have come to identify ourselves with or as, not our own images of ourselves, not our fixed characters or egos, but simply the flow of our own experience; and I mean by that chiefly what has been eliminated from it – the flow of feelings.

The whole of Primal therapy is based on the belief that we are half-creatures, that is – neurotics, because we have, in our pasts, at moments of trauma, sped from our pain into the safety of our consciousness, or mental processes. To come alive again we have to experience that pain we avoided. Pain is both the way into neurosis, and the way out of it.

I believe that it does not matter which method is adopted in order to feel again, for feeling itself is the key. If I learn or discover or am tricked into discovering how to feel again, then I do not need to unlock my memories, to relive traumas. If I can feel *now*, my relationship emotionally with all things and persons around me, feel my body, and my feelings moving within me, then I am healed, I am whole, I am my sun. Obviously unlocking memories that are extremely painful, as the primal therapists do, is an excellent method of moving a person into the realm of feeling. The same goes for Bioenergetic techniques. What is important here is the feeling experience that results, the renewal of emotional flow. The method, I maintain, is irrelevant. Meditation can do it, if used for that purpose : to reach feelings rather than to escape from them. So can a smack round the face.

We experience reality by *feeling* it, so it seems to me. But 'human kind cannot bear very much reality',[8] nor can they bear very much truth.[9] These are much the same. Both are neither good nor bad, they just *are*. It is not possible to *extract* the good and leave the bad, by some virtuous process of electrolysis. Yet, in a way, this is the aim of much psychiatry, following medicine (wherein the goal is more excusable). In

[8] T. S. Eliot, *Four Quartets*.
[9] Durrell writes, 'Perhaps our only sickness is to desire a truth which we cannot bear rather than to rest content with the fictions we manufacture out of each other' (*Clea*). Is this irony, resignation, or tragedy?

an age of science people somehow expect not to feel pain. Surely, in this space day and age, a cure exists for pain, even the pain of being oneself, the pain of grief, of guilt, of love, of hate, of really feeling, really sensing? What is science up to if it is not looking after *us* in this way? Chemotherapists pridefully rise to the bait, provide the cure: numbness, distance – from oneself as well as from the world. It would be better if we rejoiced at feeling *anything*, even if it is hate or anger or resentment or grief; for without feelings we are dead.

This flow of experience, of feeling, of energy in motion, is natural. It is man, unneurotic. Much of culture acts as a prop to neurosis because it fosters the surrogate life of the mind.

To be free to be oneself, one's self, an unlearning and a forgetting is required, a liberation from foisted patterns, a deliverance from that structured commentary on life that has for so long stood falsely for real feeling experience.

We have to see with our reason that we have to go beyond reason.

Aurobindo, the Indian sage and mystic, thus: 'Reason now demands its own transcendence.'

This is not anticultural. The best of our culture is there to be had. If we are open to but not hammered by our culture then we have a proper relationship with it. It is one thing to have our senses sharpened, another to be directed what to hear, think, see, feel, and what not to, so that our head is full of rules, injunctions and taboos.

How can we be open to the world when our head is full of enjoinders and fears? My experience is that when my head is empty I am most open to all that is around me, if I can take the terrifying risk of feeling my own nothingness.

The schizophrenic is no saint, even if he could be one in the making. The schizophrenic is not liberated, but even more imprisoned in his mind than the rest of us.

It is possible that if the state of mind so designated were left alone it could emerge into the spacious serenity of wisdom. This belief lay at the root of the Kingsley Hall experiment. Mary Barnes may be a living proof of the potential of this way.[10] I do not know. I have had too little experience of schizophrenia, outside my own borderline phases.

In PNP we met few diagnosed schizophrenics. There were some – Tiffany and Ned, whose involvement I will describe later, were both so psychiatrically diagnosed – but most are inaccessible: in hospitals, clinics and impenetrable family systems. Even were they not, they would be a tough assignment for a voluntary network like PNP. To save a schizophrenic, to return him to himself, his real energy and his life, takes tremendous commitment, skill and time, often enough. Here I do not know the *practical* answer, except that drugs, in the event, are not it.

But there is hope in this thought: Jung once said that a schizophrenic ceases to be schizophrenic when he meets someone by whom he feels understood.

If mental illness is a state of being based on infantile logic patterns reinforced by fear, and then habit, do we need experts to cure, and if so, what kind?

Psychiatrists diagnose neuroses and psychoses. Who is to diagnose the psychiatrist?

And who in turn is to diagnose *him*?

Sartre says man is the baseless base of values, since there are no absolute values against which he can measure his own. But society knows better.

The psychiatrist is the representative of social values. Psychiatry is not neutral.

Anti-psychiatry is part of a turning away from utilitarianism, the measuring of a life according to its social usefulness, towards the value of wholeness, the value of truth and what *is*, in the belief that this will lead man towards authenticity, and a life led according to a set of human values that are intrinsic and eternal.

We are stuck unless, lacking superhuman courage, we can discover or create environments in which we can *experiment*. Society offers few. Psychiatry offers the fifty-minute hour at five or more pounds a time. A few have formed their own

[10] See her recent book with Joe Berke: *Two Accounts of a Journey through Madness.*

circles, communes, groups. PNP was such a group that caught on and grew. In it there was ignorance, innocence, uncertainty and clumsiness. There was also concern, goodwill, and a minimum of mind fuck. All in all it was a fair beginning. Potentially it was unlimited, could lead to a real people's alternative to objective and objectifying psychiatry.

The need for it was quickly confirmed. Before long PNP networks sprang up outside London in Leeds, Brighton, Manchester, Stoke, Birmingham, Hull, Cardiff, Bristol and Glasgow.

To many these networks were meaningful and helpful. Often they supplied a mild haven from the family, or the social system and its pressures, or from psychiatry itself and its press-gangs.

So PNP gained a purchase, did not collapse like some innovations, did not rocket and expire like others. This was because there was a space for PNP in British society, a want, and so it educed itself out of its members.

Wheat

In London PNP grew rapidly at once. The word got around that we were functioning, whatever we were, and hundreds came to find out about this new alternative to psychiatry. Actually there was almost nothing to see or find, since those who came looking *were* PNP. The network was the people in it, that was all. For some this took a bit of swallowing, for solutions are usually looked for outside us. If we can't find it here, it must be over there. For this reason some central members were inveigled into giving a kind of therapy, but always I think with the proviso that whatever was suggested or expressed was mere opinion, without special status or authority, but no doubt some words were seized on as guides and testaments.

For many almost anything would do if it *might* help and wasn't drugs or ECT. A number had already had truck with those methods, so coarse and wide of the mark.

Many, I suppose, gained very little directly from PNP and their association with it, but psychologically they were helped by the feeling that something *could* happen, and to believe that is half-way to letting it.

So that PNP, in some ways, was a trick. It tricked many into curing themselves by making them believe that cure was possible without psychiatry.

It was as if a group of people, meeting to indict the state of theatre, provided at the meeting a new kind of show, thereby making the theatre redundant.

Others undoubtedly were helped far more directly – practically, psychologically or emotionally. We had a number come who were near the end of their tether. There was no doubt PNP often provided a lifeline, assistance back to a point where an individual could function again and cope with his life.

101

Often it was more simple than we made it. I believe that the mere existence of a PNP over a long interval of time would by itself work wonders. We nourish each other; each one of us has those he can be nourished by, those he can give nutrition to; on a spreadeagled network, with a wide variety of members, most people can find at least one person who can give them some kind of sustenance, or faith, in time of need.

For a while we were inundated. I did not complain. I had the sense of action, through others, whilst remaining inviolate, unchanged. I had fulfilled the neurotic's dream. I could talk for hours on psychiatry, neurosis, psychosis, psychoanalysis. My ideas were clear and convincing. Also I could see the neurotic patterns of others clearer even than their faces. I felt myself becoming a minor prophet. Inside, however, I remained stuck, a terrible mess.

Never mind. I did not belong to myself for a while. I had handed myself over to a cause. The cause, I see, was worthy enough. PNP was a boon. It cocked a quiet gentle snook at psychiatry, and that was due. To sacrifice myself for a while to achieve this was nothing, a bagatelle. Besides, I was eager to give myself away. At last, after almost forty years, I was getting close to myself, and the prospect of finally making it filled me with a mixture of fear, pain, horror, and devastating excitement.

PNP's quietness and gentleness made it insidious, and difficult to scotch. We met little opposition from orthodoxy. Difficult to pin down, lacking overtly much to take exception to, we functioned on innocently, like a chess club, or a group of trout-fishing enthusiasts. Eventually we were made overtures to by parts of the profession – as an ancillary phenomenon, of course. I could have been no quicker to reject any such offer of subordination. Like me, PNP would accept orders from nobody. Quite apart from this personal latency, it smacked too much of repressive tolerance : the technique of – accept, liaise, swallow, evacuate. Between an alternative, that is, a heresy, and orthodoxy, heresy must maintain a gulf – until it can negotiate on equal terms.

A small group in PNP bore the brunt of the initial avalanche. Private lives were almost swept away. Of whatever it was we were offering, the market could hardly get enough. Perhaps many were motivated merely by curiosity. Nevertheless backs began to bend under the weight. Within weeks a few were beginning to hide beyond unanswered telephones. This did not amount to abandonment, or even dereliction. There were other numbers on the list, and those most favoured were beginning to protect themselves. As flag-wallah, however, I permitted myself no such peccadilloes. I was permanently available. If I was not surely PNP would wither and die. Perhaps for a while I failed to distinguish between it and me.

But further articles in *IT*, plus natural growth, led before long to an increase in the size of the basic network, to the relief of the early pioneers. We had survived the first onslaught so well partly because this small central group had formed firm relationships. We saw one another often and became friends.

David Eddy, loyalest of friends, most conscientious of persons, offered himself to PNP at once, as nakedly as I, if less vigorously. With David you would find more space. My drift was to deal out my ideas and perceptions, which I barely distinguished from truth and reality. I had a blueprint which I handed out like mad. Not that I was a fanatic. And I rarely proselytized. It was simply that my own energy and conviction about my own view of the world was infectious. But as usual, by the time my latest credo had seized the minds of others, I was elsewhere; my beliefs now forgotten, superseded, disdained. I was the itinerant teacher *naturel*. To some : a charlatan, a damned quack. Not that quackery is without its merits. When it has them they are of the imaginative, original, inspirational kind. I see that I prefer to take my chance with them, even today, rather than with the sad dull slog of orthodoxy.

David treated his PNP visitors like princes and princesses. At the time a highly reasonable man, lecturer, writer, Good Samaritan, he believed that niceness and goodness was much, if not all. We all had limited and exaggerated gifts. Most of us have become less specific, more comprehensive, since.

103

David's gifts were patience, tolerance, understanding, and these he showered upon others like a canonized king, where they were snapped up. Around this time David was fighting to keep his marriage afloat on a basis of tolerance and controlled fury. In his PNP work he could divide this cantankerous pair, letting the Luciferic fury slip quietly away into hell, or forgetfulness. Fed by its relief from its molten companion, his tolerance became supreme. Like me, at this time, he was giving himself away in favour of others. There were many who accepted his time, his space, his intellectual energy, without hesitation. Then, my pleasure and gratitude for his tolerance, both to me and to contacts in PNP, was enormous. Today, encounteree that I am, I await with longing the bursting forth of his fury.

Mike Williamson, already introduced, thrust himself into the thick of PNP at once. He was always there, at hand. Having a lot to say, he never tired of a new audience. For months he stood in the midst of a stream of callers, never at a loss for words. He had the generosity to listen too. Moreover, like myself, he had so many conflicts at work within him that he was able to identify with most internal wars. Able to see, able to empathize, he could talk with relevance. Like me, with his own problems unsolved, he was less able to heal, at least directly. But there was the open house, the time without stint, the unceasing willingness to interact – these were of great value. Also, behind it all, there was generosity of spirit. Later, after he dropped out, and began to plough various paths of unmitigated extremism, he became temporarily paralysed by his own dark corners. Lurking beyond, always, lay an amazing creativity. In the meantime he appeared to live a hair-raising existence on the brink of desolation. Later we quarrelled. But to quarrel is not to separate, even if we are estranged. It is simply another way of relating, maintaining one of the few real bonds we are permitted in our squeezed existence.

Tarek Hassan was, in a number of ways, already an angel. He painted and wrote beautifully, played music exquisitely, and, besides, was quite beautiful to look at. Professionally he was a doctor. This I discovered much later, by accident. He had none of the airs and inflations of most doctors, with their sense of divine appointment, and their lack of openness to the shallowness and arbitrariness of the entire field of orthodox medicine. Tarek wore his skills and talents lightly. He would work hard in hospitals, and with PNP, without a sigh. Much of his energy went into concern about communication. He felt people simply did not get through to one another. Art, medicine, books – these were as nothing on the scale of complete communication, the flow of reality between persons. At the time all this flummoxed me. How could this man speak of poverty of communication in the face of my words of clarity and power? Today I understand.

Even then, not understanding, I experienced. For behind my resistance and confusion there was, above all, a flow of love between us.

There were four women in that first fifteen. One was Alma Davies. Quietly, she became a key figure in the network. Having a presence, she was looked for in her absence. She was a face on a fountain that provides drink but which itself needs to drink. She was a creature of quiet flow. Silently, wordlessly, she would change decisions without a word. Casting a spell, she would fall under others. Tarek, David, much later myself, all played with her this spelling game. In the early days of PNP she was much in demand. Being a woman, young and attractive, many hoped they could solve their sexual hangups through talking and being with her. Often overwhelmed by numbers, she would cry for help. Finally she fled to Bali. Later she returned, to some of us but not to PNP.

But the very first to join was Tom. He burst in on me the very morning *IT* with my article hit the streets, brandishing the paper, and explained to me what had happened. 'Mike, you realize what this is all about, don't you? You've discovered God.' My bumbling hesitations were swept aside. 'Of course you have, old boy. This whole article reeks of it. This is marvellous! I want to know exactly how it happened. I've got to know. It's terrific!'

In the pub, over tonic waters, he elaborated matters. PNP

was just right. The whole world was waiting. I would have a full-scale movement on my hands, of monstrous proportions. I felt myself sinking, quietly, into nothingness. I was aware of my weakness, my impotence; it was not for me to be called. Over the smoke and bubbles Tom weaved his patterns of history. With a jab of his forefinger he indicated the critical threshold – *now*. Enter PNP. It was God-given, to be God-directed. The world would follow. It was inevitable. PNP having just taken its bow, was now disappearing before my eyes; in its place – a religious crusade. I was way out of my depth. I felt weak and tiny, an impossible prophet. I made myself numb, as I would as a child. Tom, blazing eyes blind and undaunted, bore me aloft, my feet thrashing feebly. I could not call on God since He was clearly on Tom's side.

It went on and on, until I could keep numb no longer. Instead I let it happen, I let go, and then magically I was on dry land, with Tom's words lapping lightly over me, leaving me intact. Finally he swept out striding, his head high, the fire of the future new psychiatry ablaze in his eyes, leaving me drained, yet with my PNP intact – and my first recruit.

Another woman in that first team was Jenny James. To be honest Jenny's letter had frightened me :

'Please write to me. I want to help, will do anything, from typing to blowing up psychiatrists.'

What was all this? I wanted a good clean movement; no fights, no CAPA deals. Besides, I had not yet forgotten how to be a gentleman – at my mother's behest. Nevertheless we met. She was an old campaigner, Jenny, a veteran of CND and other various protests. She listened to my plans with high excitement, peeing frequently – a sure sign, she said. At that first meeting we all had, she left early. Impatient with words, she practically equated life with action – a fallacy and an evasion, as Rimbaud saw.[1] This was *her* exaggeration – and her gift to PNP. Time and again she saved the day with her imme-

[1] 'Action is not life, but a way of spoiling some kind of force, an enervation.'

diacy. In addition she was indefatigable. Today, four and a half years later, queen of PNP house, she lives at the hub of throngs, and alone of the original fifteen remains still in the movement.

Probably, over the years, Jenny has done more in and for PNP than anybody. Many hundreds have graced, or ungraced, PNP house since she moved in – the first tenant. In addition, for two years now, along with her close friend Jerry Rothenberg, she has held free Encounter groups at the house, of a very high calibre. What's more, beyond her action, she gives to all she knows an honesty and directness as shockingly refreshing as a jet of cold water.

Not quite to all. I, at least, am excluded. She reacts to our conflicts, which have been neither trivial nor infrequent, by withdrawing into a smouldering anger. With me, somehow, she cannot let go her left hook. I too am guilty. When we meet, which is rarely now, we fight out our war in silence. For her, I suspect, I have the uncommon status of a failed hero. Founder of PNP, I had the sauce to be weak and faulty. Obsessed with equality, Jenny failed to forgive me for not being exceptional.

Never mind. We both functioned separately and in peace. Up to a point, Jerry, whom we both love, keeps us apart. For when we are together, both of us relate easily to him, thereby avoiding confrontation with each other. Nevertheless, avoiding each other, we relate together intensely. The Gestalt between us is far from closed. In the meantime I have the highest respect for her. I am not satisfied with this. I should like to love her.

Right from the beginning we had help from behind the enemy's lines. Three of the original fifteen, Tarek excluded, were professionals in the system. This proportion, a fifth, was always at least maintained. It gives some hope for the system.

Frank McAllan was a mental health officer. Among his duties was that of visiting families with a disturbed member, and either smoothing things over, maintaining equilibrium, or arranging for intervention, such as hospitalization. There was a lot he could do to avoid the excesses of the system; despite this, a quasi-Laingian approach, and the depth of his own sensibility, Frank frequently found his work and its effects distressing. Actions were forced upon him not of his choosing. This was inevitable. You cannot work behind the lines and constantly rebel. True colours have to be partly camouflaged or you lose your footing.

Nevertheless Frank ploughed on, maintaining a discreet balance, and giving time, off-duty, to PNP.

Once he tested out the network as a possible extension of his organized activity. He sent a young man who was in a mess in his rigid family field to Tom and his girl-friend Joan. In three days that man saw more of life than he had in years. Fresh vistas opened, rolling to new horizons. It was a disaster, like giving a prisoner the full treatment of a night on the town on his one short parole, before returning him to prison to complete a life sentence.

Tom was partly to blame, of course. Lacking acumen and niceness, he failed to feel his way. But this apart, the episode shows the difficulties in using PNP as an auxiliary to orthodoxy. The worlds are different. PNP stands not only for an alternative to psychiatry, but for a new way of life. Most of those who come to PNP are already practising new modes of being and relating, to an extent. As a result PNP jells easily. But for those living in tight fixed situations, that subject them strongly to social pressures, moralities and expectations, PNP is a strong draught, or remote. To experience PNP, and get benefit from it, people may need to go overboard, and probably they, and certainly PNP, are not prepared for that.

At the same time, behind the activity of PNP, there was the offer of a new environment :

'Roughly, PNP is an attempt to take an individual psychiatric problem into a fresh group-setting. The argument can be put thus : if one (localized) environment acting on an individual can – along with other factors – produce a kind of sickness, or at least self-defeating activity, why shouldn't an alternative (localized) environment be able, to an extent, to right things and set the individual's organism burgeoning again? To put it another way : an individual forms part of an environmental field, set up by himself and others. The field is created by the relationships of these people to each other. It then proceeds to act on each one of them, determining the part each must play in the interaction. This part can be that of "schizo-phrenic", "master", "slave", "freak", and so on. But if those playing the parts of "losers" are offered a new field, they may find they can act in new and more positive ways. Even if it is merely a different way, this in itself can provide a huge relief.'[2]

But it was far from being a total environment, so that as a complete alternative it was wanting, this PNP. We could not supply circumferential support; but we could supply one com-ponent of a loose environment for those in search of a way of life based on personal space and individual liberty.

What Frank had sought through PNP, through Tom, was an alternative to hospital for the person encased in a family system that was proving personally pernicious. For such a person the door is no way out,[3] at least not if he must take it alone. Where can the lost and dependent go, to escape from pathogenic surroundings? At worst, the person could share the fate of Gribouille, who, to avoid getting wet in the rain, jumped into the river and drowned. But at best – I don't know. Even the recuperative benefits of hospitalization, one of its rare treats, are being lost in the rush for snap cures. Get them in; dose them up; then get them out and back to the grind – that is the current trend. Today, even psychiatry swings.

And I remember when I read Laing and Esterson's *Sanity, Madness and the Family* how dismayed I was at the fact that all those poor women would end up by being returned to bosoms of families which, like Cleopatra's, concealed an asp.

A complete alternative here would amount to an alternative society. In some ways it seems a pity we do not use trans-

[2] From the article, 'People Not Psychiatry', by the author, published in *New Society*, 31 December, 1970.

[3] 'The way out is via the door. Why is it that no one will use this method?' (Confucius). Laing uses this as his epigraph in *The Self and Others*.

People, Not Psychiatry

portation any more, for so-called misfits. What a chance that would be for those trapped between the Scylla of the mental hospital and the Charybdis of family life!

Jim S., another pro amongst us, was a psychiatric nurse. He provided us with a number of hair-raising stories about life in his hospital, in particular concerning the use of ECT punitively, to control difficult and recalcitrant patients. Because he opted out of this nefarious game, Jim had been ostracized by his colleagues. Lacking the confidence to make a stand, he stewed instead. Subduing his anger and his disgust, he became very miserable. Lacking friends amongst his equals, he sought for them amongst us and PNP. He was depressed, too, by the co-operation of patients in this regime. Offered the role of victim, many of them accepted, for it gave them an identity at a time when they felt lost. But a hospital sub-universe, the field of staff and patient interaction, once created by its members, wheels round and dictates. And such a field tends towards stasis. The natural dynamic of individuals is lost to the forces of field maintenance and equilibrium.

This institutional stasis reflects of course current psychiatric perspective. We live in a psychiatric era of theory and behavioural and chemical equations. Modes of cure are mechanistic or cerebral, rather than experiential. 'The cause of this is this.' 'Ah yes, that means this is so.' Or worse: 'If we do this to the patient, this happens.' 'Inject this; the result – this.' Everything is either rationalistic or empirical – opposite poles with no centre: a typically Western phenomenon.

Theoretically we continue to groan under the yoke of Freud. For Freud, affects were precipitates of 'primeval traumatic experiences'. He likened them to hysterical seizures. Most people continue to do so today. Many individuals who come to Encounter groups complain that they can find *nowhere* to shout or scream or cry. What hostages we give to society! We send people to Bedlam and there they live out our rhapsodies and our rages and our terrors for us.

But a new age of pathology is already heralded. Nor is it limited to psychological ills. It will lead to an entirely new orientation towards physical sickness too. It is hard to con-

110

ceive how we could have gone so long treating different aspects of man independently.

Experience is seen to be both the cause of sickness – even if it is reinforced and concreted by the mind – and also the path of cure. It is fitting that many of these new methods should be implemented in what are known as 'workshops'. To work, here, is to undergo experiences with the whole self, probably with the body active, definitely participating, and certainly with feelings aflow.

Feelings are the key. They are the soul's instruments of experience. Observation is nothing, without an emotive counterpart. Feelings flow, as life should; but thought and logic do not. They may last a lifetime, cripple us, make us rigid and fettered, gripped by an idea.

If I am free to feel, and express, hate for you, or rage at you, I shall be free to perhaps love you or praise you later. But if I deny my feelings, or change their status to that of *facts*, so that they become fixed, then the feelings are stuck, and I am stuck with them.

These are the two poles : denial of feelings and reification of feelings. At both poles there is no movement; the feelings are blocked. Health, the flow of life, of our own life, lies in the centre.

When we disown our feelings, or are subtly governed by them through their conversion into static facts, we are neurotic. At the root of all neuroses lies fear of feelings, and consequent alienation from them. We fear their force, their overwhelming nature, their giddy fluctuations, their very flow – which threatens our cosy notions of a permanent identity, and we fear the pain; and so we hang on to our sanforized, safe, mechanical worlds, and along with them to the painful feelings themselves, which, remaining in us, disrupt our lives.

It is my belief that the pain has to be felt in order to properly live. Otherwise we place our lives on a slab from which we study the world – without belonging to it.

But all this barely belongs to this dying age of a dried-up rationality, too often divorced from feelings and from body needs.

Many psychiatrists and psychotherapists distrust feelings. They fear anarchy, irrationality, the Bacchanalian whirl; they fear for civilization and a stable social system. But often the truth of the matter is that they are afraid of feelings because they do not know how to handle them. Rarely having fully felt their own, they know little of the emotional immersion experience. How then can they guide? Nor can they let be. In psychotherapy, in hospitals, patients are constantly fished out of their feelings and thrust back into their heads in order to talk *about*. But talking about misses the mark. It is not living, but a commentary on it. It fails to involve us; rather does it leave us behind. It removes us from the scene. It turns us, life actors and life actresses, into *critics* at our crucial moments.

How else can we account for the widespread refusal of orthodox practitioners in this country to have any truck whatsoever with the Encounter movement and its techniques other than as testimony to their fear?

Early in 1972 I was interviewed by two very senior members of a psychotherapy institute. I had put in a tentative application for studentship a year or so before, largely at the instigation of my current therapist, D. By this time I was hardly interested at all, but, clownishly, I thought the institute might be useful for referrals.

At the time of the interview – I had already had several – I was running Encounter groups. I was informed that if I was accepted as a student I would on no account be allowed to earn my money to pay fees in this way. I would have to sever all connection with the movement. Oh, brave seigneurs! They themselves were already 'finding out who our friends are'. Certain members had made links of one sort or another with the new movement and its methods. These were to be asked to give an assurance of total fealty to either Jung or Freud and to break all connection with the Encounter world and its techniques; or to resign. Between the institute and the Human Potential movement there was to be a gulf. No bridge; and passage prohibited.

They went on: the training was Freudian or Jungian.

They did not want 'awkward students who questioned things all the time'. They were offering a choice of two bodies of knowledge and they wanted students who would accept one or other of them without challenging the basic assumptions on which it rested.

Out of this interview came a remark for the annals. P., a Jungian and one of the interviewers, said this about Fritz Perls, 'I've just finished reading his book. In it he really wipes the floor with psychoanalysis.' She shook her head, and added, 'He must have had a very poor analysis himself.'

That is being locked up in a symbolic universe, from which all can be explained. We are the truth, and if you do not accept it, no matter; we can explain you away. Such persons are not purveyors of life, but of places in a gazebo. Entry by way of a total ideology. If you want a testament, you could try shopping there, amongst the analysts. But if you prefer life and flow to explanation and theory, you should keep well clear of them.

This stand places the student therapist in a tricky position. He needs one association or another in order to formally qualify, and each insists on more or less total conformity to a party line. Recognized officially, they hold all the cards – and make all the rules, one of which, as I discovered, was no personal methodology, no innovation.

If impregnable castles cannot be breached, they have to be made obsolete. This is going to be Freudianism's fate. And the sooner the better. It is far too heavy-handed. Freud was a man who invented an elaborate game. Like chess it has fascinated millions. Let others play it, and if these others teach it to yet others who want to learn it, well and good; it *might* even be therapeutic. But don't let us raise this game to the status of a therapeutic law. Let it be played in dark corners, but let other quicker, more direct and more experiential methods take the spotlight and the stage. It is time.

I have had my experience of both fringe and mainstream psychotherapy, and I have had my gain and profit from them. I am aware, now that I am on the other side of the deal, how hard it is to assess this profit, change, growth, progress made, call it what you will. For the vantage point from which we presume to measure is not outside time. Like a fly in a train, our view of ourselves moves with us. In this work ingratitude is rife. Marty Fromm[4] calls it the game of 'shoot the therapist'. Gratitude too is common enough, yet appreciation is far from being a valid scale on which to award garlands. I see now that I got far more from my visits to my first therapist, P., than I ever conceded at the time. He started the whole thing going for me – the struggle to free myself from the morass in my head. Through him I saw that my world of fantasy and cerebration was not real at all. Through him I *experienced* my schizoid state. Well and good. In the first place he was far from a conventional worker. Next, I believe there are quicker ways of making the same gains. A difference I see between psychotherapy and the new methods like Gestalt, Psychofantasy, Bioenergetics and Encounter is this : in psychotherapy it is very possible *to waste time* (and therefore money); in the new approaches, with their emphasis on the here-and-now and continual awareness, whatever happens – nothing, boredom, verbalization, evasion – is brought into the awareness continuum *and becomes an experience of self.*

After returning to P. for a while I gave up therapy. This coincided with the setting up of PNP. The following year was the most disastrous and devastating year emotionally, yet I never felt the need to consult anybody. Possibly I would have seen it as treason. In any case I prefer help more to get myself flowing than as support or aid in time of stress or despair.

When I began again having therapy my motives seemed different : I saw in another what I wanted for myself and believed that by setting up a therapeutic relationship with him I would gain what he had : by osmosis? apeing? identification? learning? I don't know, but I believed it would happen and it did. What I was after was the capacity to say 'Bullshit!' when I wanted to, when I felt it in my guts, at a difficult time.

It happened like this : I was present at a meeting at which Tom Scheff, a well-known Californian therapist and sociolo-

---

[4] An American Gestalt therapist, loved one of the late Fritz Perls. See his *In and Out of the Garbage Pail.*

gist, was presenting for the first time in this country the method of Re-evaluation Counselling – a lay form of therapy between peers. Tom was very convincing, a good and energetic speaker, and yet at the time I felt unhappy in my heart about the whole approach.[5] All I seemed to be able to muster however were a few niggling queries on details, which Tom consummately demolished. Yet I was far from satisfied. Inside, I wanted to blow up. What was I blocking? Then at the far end of the room a voice said, 'That's bullshit.' Very quietly, very firmly. The silence was electric. Tom looked a bit taken aback. As for me, I was stunned with excitement, my heart pounding. I wanted that, to be able to say Bullshit when I felt it, to say it spontaneously in the face of my fear. Not that I was always chicken, but I knew I chose my times to be brave. When it really came to it, when it was really hard, I withdrew, cut off, went silent and numb, or sat squirming on my dynamite keg.

When it was all over, soon after, I sped like an arrow to this brave archer and asked him if he would give me therapy.

He was a member of an institute. I went to him twice weekly for nine months and I also attended two groups a week which he, D., took with L. It was L. who scolded me for my aggression in a group in an incident I mentioned earlier.

I spent a lot of my time with him trying to make out what was happening in him to make him the way he was. I suppose I wanted that 'bullshit' badly. Also, I couldn't stop playing the therapist just because I was a patient. The idea was that I lie on the couch and talk freely. Rarely did the words come in a flow; and if I was reluctant to lie down, if I wanted to sit in a chair or on the floor, or move around, this was interpreted as my fear he would rape me. When a therapist throws his world at you like that, and you have abdicated your own strength sufficiently to see yourself as a patient and in need

[5] I have far fewer doubts now about this mode of reciprocal therapy, or self-disclosure. It can be extremely powerful, if limited, and I was very impressed by, and liked, its originator, Harvey Jackin, when I met him. It has the advantages of costing nothing, and being open to all. For a full description see Harvey Jackin, *The Human Side of Human Beings*.

of help, it can really thrust you into some dark corners, whether they really exist or not.

He became impatient because the transference wouldn't take. He couldn't make up *his* mind whether for me he was my mother, father or brother. For a while – this is an occupational hazard of being a patient – I discussed this with him seriously, really bothered by the uncertainty. I began to get angry with myself for not plumping for one or another; I was holding up the therapy. Finally I told him, in a fit of autonomy, that to me he was just D. 'Come, come, Michael,' he said, 'Do you think you are different from everyone else? There is *always* a transference.'

Most of the nine months seemed to be spent in trying to cram as much of me into him as possible,[6] so that he would *understand* me. Once that was done, presumably he would begin to sort me out for me.

In order to hasten this initial objective, I suppose, he used an elaborate system of symbols. For instance, one of my eyes, to him, was my mother's vagina, the other was my father's anus. I grappled with that flabbergasting fact for a while, finally concluding that it was completely useless to me, though perhaps vital to D. and the trip he was on with me.

Finally I told him I thought he was mad. There was a heavy pause. Then he said, 'You don't really believe that, do you?' Pause. 'Yes,' I said, 'I do.'

Then I told him I thought his Freudian interpretations were mostly crap and his symbolism so much bullshit.

I had got what I wanted. The therapy was over.

Therapy naturally ends when the patient finds from himself what he seeks from the therapist.[7]

I got other things too. I liked D. a lot. He would make a fine group leader. In the meantime I feel he has sold out. But perhaps he is working for change from the inside.

Most therapy is a game. The therapist interprets the patient – his history and his behaviour – in terms of his own

[6] I can imagine his eyes lighting up as he reads this. So all the time it was I who wanted to rape him!

[7] My ability to say bullshit! when I feel it, has not been lost!

116

symbolic universe, and feeds this to the patient who, having already forsaken his own centre, accepts this symbolic world as a means of making sense of his own experience. Therapy ends when the patient either buys the universe completely, perhaps becoming a therapist himself, or when he recovers contact with his own self, his own feeling and sense of who he is and what the world means to him, so that he begins to interpret, or at least see, the therapist in terms of *his* universe.

In the new group therapies, the individual member is not harassed by the group leader's interpretations, and the leader's view of 'what's going on' in the member, whilst often offered, is merely a commentary, or margin notes, to the individual's actual experience. The mind is not central to the therapy, but nor is it outcast; it is, hopefully, joined to praxis, to physical and emotional flow of experience.

I do not begin to put these methods forward as a panacea, as *the* way. But together they amount to a brave – and effective – attempt to tackle neuroses at their root, both in the past and in action in the here and now. Each method moves individuals towards maximization of self-awareness, self-responsibility and self-support. It is not a tender package. It includes often awareness of that despair that Kierkegaard maintained lies at the heart of every man. It can often be detected on the faces of group leaders, this despair. But then the Danish philosopher also said that the worst kind of despair is not to know that one is in despair, so awareness scores again.

The Human Potential movement is not peddling a soft paradise. It markets the lines of total responsibility for oneself, complete openness to experience, and maximum awareness of oneself. It also takes the stand that one's experience derives from within oneself and not from outside agents who 'do things to us'.

I would like to end this chapter here with Fritz Perls' 'Gestalt Prayer'. It seems fitting. It also makes a charming finale :

> I do my thing, and you do your thing.
> I am not in this world to live up to
> > your expectations

And you are not in this world to live
> up to mine.
You are you and I am I,
And if by chance we find each other,
> it's beautiful.
If not, it can't be helped.[8]

[8] From *Gestalt Therapy Verbatim.*

Leaf

Like new territory we were explored; searched for needs : for sex, succour or solidarity, for love, solace, for understanding, for truth and for confirmation, for acceptance and for friendship, for the answers to the overwhelming questions, for what was lacking in lives, in persons. And all the time we were being tested : could we, he, she, be trusted?

Trust plays a big part in change. We seize up because we stop trusting our own flow, and that, when we are young, is often the same as ceasing to trust another – father, mother, etc. – or others. To flow again, from a blocked state, probably involves a trust in others, with and through whom there can be experimentation.

As I have said, infantile logic patterns lie at the root of blocked and distorted lives, or neuroses. But I believe there is a natural force within us thrusting us back towards flow and growth. Our potential remains, invisibly contained in our seed, driving towards fulfilment.

Sometimes, like a wicked winter, the environment deals harshly with that open free-flowing organism – the human child. The plant, attacked by ice and frost, or drought, or a savage wind, can do little more than fight for its life, survive strengthened, or die. But the human has other methods to protect himself : he can shrink, go numb, cut off from the reality of the deadly climate. He can find a clearing – in his head – into which he can retire, and pretend that his experience *isn't really happening*.

But the price paid is extravagant; the pain of feeling is eventually eclipsed, monumentally, by the pain of not feeling, for this is a pain of the soul.

To change this situation is not easy. In the first place there are the fears of letting go what has, at least, kept one alive, and moving into unknown territory, where 'one' is no longer in control (then who is?), and therefore anything may happen. The catastrophic expectations of being oneself, going with the flow from moment to moment. Would I go mad, be outlawed, despised, rejected, locked up?

What is more, the human being, quite naturally, *makes the best of a bad job*. We all make capital out of our neuroses. Often we wake up to find ourselves unfree, incomplete, unreal, and then proceed to harvest what we can from the blighted crop. We use our situation to get what we want, and to manipulate others.

To change all this, to surrender our neuroses, involves giving up everything, starting again. We have to be reborn, or rather allow ourselves to become again the being we truly are: a stranger, sometimes; at other times the reality to the simulacrum we have been.

Often unawares, and with varying energy, we search for settings in which we can experiment, take risks, move for a spell out of the cage that imprisons us, and at the same time protects us.

In part, no doubt, I created PNP for this purpose. In fact, when it came to the crunch, to my own personal crisis, I could not use it, as I shall relate. But many did. PNP was a move towards providing *natural* settings in which experiments with oneself and one's relationships could be made, in which trust could develop to this end.

Despite the existence of an infrastructure – the set of names on the floating lists – reciprocity and peer group exchange were the bases of PNP. It happened that those who visited gave power to their hosts; it happened that those at home to visitors assumed power, or tried to; but as time went on, artificial standings became, on the whole, eliminated. Finally, after my personal influence on dynamics decreased, anybody could have his or her name on the list, by request, so that the collation grew to hundreds. By this time the shape of PNP was no longer how I had drafted it out, and envisaged it growing. For better or worse, it was different, and at least it made real the

stand that there is no such thing as mental sickness, that
sanity is always relative, person to person, and never absolute,
in a way that many who take that stand, intellectually, omit
to live out actually, in practice.

Current notions of health tend to be based on concepts of
'the average' – which strikes me as absurd; should we not
rather base it on the exceptional, on those who have realized
greater degrees of the human potential?

To do this, to risk increasing potential, from a position of
safety, of sensible, compromising, controlled and suppressed
normality, may entail a spell of 'going crazy'. The very same
state, alarming, threatening, and inexplicable to the settled
sane and their protectors, the psychiatrists, may mark the
advent of a serious emotional breakdown *or* the beginnings
of a breakthrough into new realms of personal growth and
freedom.[1]

Being a therapist involves humility, for the flow of shared
experience can be indubitably both ways, if the therapist,
surrendering the temptation to see himself as a source of truth
and wisdom and in need of nothing from the patient, who in
any case is in no position to offer him a thing, can be open
to his petitioner, the patient, so that what takes place between
these two persons in this most electrifying of meetings, does
so in 'the between', so that both are affected, and we do
not have one person, O.K. and unchanging, 'fixing' another,
with all the opportunity for manipulation and abuse that
brings – not to mention the complacency and the arrogance
intrinsic in such a stance.

'We go beyond some of our colleagues who have stated that
"schizophrenia" holds some secrets of the unconscious, and hold
that *only* psychosis contains the key to the vastness and grandeur of the deepest levels of the unconscious.'[2]

Working in PNP it became obvious many times that the
emotionally distressed, whether in the throes of change or of

[1] This ambiguity is pointed out by Assigioli, *Psychosynthesis*, and also
by Aristotle.
[2] J. N. Rosen, *Direct Analysis*.

disastrous patterns, were closer to the mainspring of some sides of life, and that they knew much of hidden human forces that most of us disown. This is not to make saints or heroes out of them, for they find these riches (and horrors) within them in part because they cannot get them from the world around them; then once hooked on to this alternative reality, they lose touch with shared human reality, of which they become terrified, and as a result miss out on meaningful activity in this shared world; activity made more meaningful because it *is* shared.

Quite a high proportion – perhaps a third – of those who made contact with PNP had experience as patients in State psychiatry. Few had a good word to say for any of it. (By contrast it was not uncommon for therapists to be well spoken of.) Here is a verbatim account from one individual. It is fairly typical :

'I took an overdose and woke up in a mental hospital. I felt I had just been through the most devastating experience of my life, but in the hospital I was just another sick patient. The staff were only interested in running the hospital – administration, food, cleaning, the timetable. And of course the dishing out of pills. I was given handfuls but nobody would tell me what they were or what they were for. I felt myself becoming an imbecile, or a thing. I saw a psychiatrist for a few minutes about once a week, and he spent this giving me his latest diagnosis. One week it was manic-depressive, the next neurotic obsessional, the next schizophrenic. When I asked for therapy he laughed, said all that was old-fashioned. Then I had ECT. I don't know how many times. That period is still foggy. After it I used to lie in bed in a blank dream. Then I was discharged as cured. Before I went in, taking the overdose and all that, I couldn't see much point in living. I thought – either I'm missing out on it, or I just don't like it. I don't feel any different now. Perhaps being part of PNP will help.'

The first letter I ever received on behalf of PNP, the first of many hundreds, was from Shirley, sixteen, in a psychiatric wing of a hospital. Here are some extracts from it :

'I've just read your article in *IT* on psychiatry and wow, did I need that! Jesus I thought I was just stupid or something, or just all wrong. Although I think you're a bit overcritical, I think you've really hit it in places. . . . One has, I think, before getting on the psychiatry scene, a lovely warm idea of friendly psychiatrists and nurses in mental hospitals, who'll be kind and warm etc. Surprise! they're the most fucked up load of squares I've ever come across, in other words biased and sometimes downright unfriendly human beings. Not all though, but some are.

'All I want to do with my life is . . . create and communicate and how can one get through to greys about this kind of thing? . . . If you could see the load of self-centred, self-pitying whining bunch in here! . . . I just sit there screaming. . . .

'Right now I have three alternatives of living, home (must be kidding), this place, or running away, in which case the fuzz would just grab me . . . the only alternative is suicide, and that's a bad trip, I want to live. I'm just bloody trapped by time; my parents try to shoulder the blame when I do anything wrong, take on my own responsibilities. It makes me mad. And when I was seeing a psychiatrist as an outpatient once again my parents hung round my neck with "what did he say?" and "how do you feel?" I just want to be left alone to fight it out. I know I need help that's why I've managed somehow to stay at this place (so far) but the actual *real* help one gets is so little compared to the "go there", "do this", and the general "we're all straights and what the hell are you" scene. That kind of attitude just makes me miserable. . . . If they shoved me in with a load of articulate intelligent heads I'd get somewhere faster than here, so that's where your new scene sounds good, this place is such one *hell* of a price for the little real help one gets. Which is why I'm on a permanent dividing line between walking out and staying.'

I went to see her a couple of times. We walked the corridors, sometimes strolled outside. It seemed absurd to me, her being here, in a hospital for the sick. She was lively, intelligent, brimming with energy, and, like so many, robbing herself of enjoying all this with consuming thoughts of 'where she was at', wondering whether or not she was mad, all fermented by the fact that she was where she was – in mental hospital. Psychiatry contributes to the very conditions it exists to cure.[3]

Of course she was at war with her parents, but this struggle is as old as man – and healthy, not sick. We all have to cut the cord to become what we are.

Shirley had smoked pot, crime of crimes, and her parents had found out. They had used this to get Shirley accepted as in need of psychiatric help. They had elicited the help of the State in their fight to control Shirley and to enforce upon her their own ideas of what's right and what's wrong.

All's fair I suppose, in war, even the one against our own children; more so perhaps, since this war involves that other proverbially lawless struggle – love. Children, to outwit those fading, rapacious dragons – parents, need to invent a new strategy, based on solidarity, cunning, and unremitting resistance, for they will never, until they are strong, beat their parents at their own games based on attachment, duty, and sweet reason.

Even supposing Shirley was confused, distressed, and suffering (she certainly wasn't dangerous to anyone, or anywhere near deeply disturbed), mental hospital seems, from a universally human if not from a societal point of view, to be completely inappropriate. Really, what can pills and ECT and a busy staff, in any case mostly dyed in the wool, do for a young girl searching for her own centre and sense of independence? At least a network like PNP seems to be on the right lines in situations like this.

In the meantime, we need to be aware of the existence of a *politics* of psychiatry, of psychiatry as a political instrument used to protect and perpetuate a fixed morality and a *status quo*.

In due course Shirley left the hospital and went to the West Country alone, spent six months there, roaming around, act-

[3] As, of course, does civilization itself.

ing independently, and came back a woman. Soon she got a job working in the Community Services. Like us all, she had reached a new level of maturity through her own experience, and her own flow.

Ra! Ra! Ra! Bang the drum. But beware. And turn a deaf ear if you want to. And don't quote me, for I am likely to disagree with you if you do.

Still, the fight for change seems always worth waging, even if society seems as mad as ever before, so that even if in the past the children have won, as parents they seem to have done no better.

But perhaps victory goes only to the few, to those who escape the clutches of contemporary insanity and yet avoid the grips of the new madness. The narrow road between them that leads through independence and self-support to health and maturity is paved with pillory, pitfall and crucifixion. Not to mention pain and despair. Never mind, it's the only way worth taking, and besides, if the East is right about *Karma* and rebirth we shall keep coming back until we do.

I do not speak of the way of the saint; nor of those of the fakir or the yogi. I am talking of *the way of emotional honesty* and the acceptance of full responsibility for what one is. I have this feeling that this kind of honesty and self-acceptance leads eventually to a life of truth, flow and compassion, and *that*, as a goal, forgotten as soon as thought of, and never to be realized, seems right enough to me.

I see that Fritz Perls writes:

'I believe we are living in an insane society and that you only have the choice either to participate in this collective psychosis or to take risks and become healthy and perhaps also crucified.'[4]

Out of the shoals of letters I have picked a few more. Many were brief and to the point, like these two from James in Birkenhead and from Laraine in London.

'Two weeks ago I felt I ought to offer help to people. Today, I need help – I think. Tomorrow, who knows? In any case,

[4] From *Gestalt Therapy Verbatim.*

125

I had to write to you. I'm 28, married/separated, bread no problem. Tell me about it.'

'You letter in *IT* – thank you.[5] Am getting frightened by a sort of growing tightness inside – something to do with block in communication, getting worse. Would like to get involved/help/be helped.'

A woman bottles herself up because, for one reason, she has ceased to trust herself; behind that lies fear, the fear of the world's (her mother/father) reaction to her if she were to flow, feel, express herself. To believe that such existential states of being can be altered and changed to ones of flow, through the application of chemicals, strikes me as senseless, a characteristic of blinkered scientism.

Some of the letters received were nightmarish and full of terror. Yet they were often beautiful too. Again the link between terror and beauty, caught by Rilke. Here is part of a letter from a young schoolgirl in Essex :

'When people are totally aware of the position they are in, i.e. horror, *terror*, stark raving naked CONSCIOUSNESS etc., *then it is possible to give to others who are ready to receive.*

'However, due to lack of funds I am unable to appreciate that which is created for me by giving minds. If my creative spirit can be fed perhaps I can give to others in some way, and create something. . . . Beauty should be free, music should be free.

'Since I started taking ACID I am unable to continue living and I am asking your advice as to the future use of the drug.

'I have had a vision of Heaven and Hell. . . . Am I one voice amongst many who are the same as I? Am I a ripple on the ocean who can never be helped, or are there superior human beings who can help me along the way? I look to you to save me in some way by giving me advice.

[5] Refers to a later contribution to *IT*, as does some of the other material quoted in this chapter.

'My consciousness stands naked and I have become aware of a country so vast that my conscious mind just cannot cope with the knowledge of it.

'Do you think that it is wise that a drug, such as Acid, should be let loose on an ignorant mass who are unable to control its usage? On the other hand, the argument goes that people must be aware, must have a vision of horror to be ready to give and create etc.

'Television and the whole mass media are evil. They are the forces of evil which are leading the blind. The blind sit and listen and have their sleeping consciousnesses battered upon by these forces. . . .

'. . . These are the words of the horror scene :

conditioned	circle
robot	fate
conditioned reflex	SYSTEM
predetermination	pattern

'I am not saying I am superior to these blind people – I am blind myself. This is the terror – I am aware of being blind. How can I integrate these two sides of myself –

1. my awareness of the futility of my existence with
2. my existence?

'In other words when I am in a state of somnambulism "my vision" is repressed into the unconscious and I am unaware of it BUT it exists somewhere in that vast country called Psyche and possesses an energy which it exerts in some way, the effect of which is disrupting my life. . . .

'The Position of *Books* in Society/civilization today has been elevated beyond proportion. A person is living in many worlds at once, one of these being the world of books. . . . People communicate through each other. This is why I write to you – personally. . . .

'I think that the biggest problem of the coming years is the population explosion. With so many people, communication must be made SOMEHOW. People are rubbing shoulders with each other, each one an island defended by super-ego and influenced greatly by the environment they find themselves in.

'Letting our grown-up pride hide all the need inside. People who need People.

. . . When it comes to everyday living such as food, job, clothes, place to live in etc. – I break down and cling to the skirts of my mother.

'Life is choosing. WILL or WILL NOT.

'I choose to love my mother

'I choose to have a love scene, to give, to create

'I choose the feelings I entertain in my mind

'I choose to be afraid

but this choice is influenced and guided by external environment. . . . I want to change the environment I live in but I cannot. . . . I cannot do it alone.

'My mistake was to have taken acid because I am not ready for the bombshell that has been delivered.

'Everything I ever lived for before is now an illusion. My whole past life is now an illusion. *The vision of horror* – the horror is the futility. Is this real or is it an illusion?

Dear Mike,

I would be most grateful if you would reply to this letter. The most important question I have to ask is this :

' *"The futility and endlessness of the horror vision* – this circling, systematic pattern of existence, with predetermined moves and its whole aura of inevitability. *Is this real? Or is it an illusion in my mind?"*

IS IT real?

'I hope you know what I'm talking about. If you do not know. . . . I'm sorry to trouble you but would you please give me a reply to that effect. This is important and is rocking my very life foundations.

'If it is true, I refuse to believe it or have a part of it, therefore am I a lost soul?

'I have become aware of two realities. One is internal the other is external. With the internal vision I can cope. Is this external vision true? Is it real? If you have *had* the external vision *please* tell me.

'Has IT visited you?

'If it has please, please, help me as I cannot live.'

This is a beautiful letter. Most of it comes from a source recognizable at once as real and true. It is very moving because it is obvious that the writer, N., has really *experienced* what she has written, so that in turn we really experience her words. This is one of the arts of good poetry – the raising of the act of reading to that of affective experience. Unless we feel, our experience does not affect us; it is as if it is happening to another, or in a vacuum.

It is frightening to imagine the possible reactions among psychiatrists, teachers, doctors and social workers to material like this.

It probably gives grounds for committal. A psychiatrist I know read it and said at once 'schizophrenia'.

Yet there is nothing in it pathological or foreign to me, or to many others. Fortunately N. picked one of us to write to.

PNP has frequently helped those suffering from the effects of bad acid trips. Later it even had 'specialists' in this work. But 'help' is not therapy, not hot towels and cold compresses and comfort, with pills of forgetfulness. It amounts to a further look at the experience and the reactions to it with others who have shared something similar.

Over and over again we had people come to us in PNP who had 'seen', become aware of, experienced, some deep truth about themselves, about living in society, and could not bear it, could not bear, that is, knowing a truth so blatantly unseen or disregarded by others; being alone amongst those that they knew – as far as they knew – in that knowledge.

But of course most people don't want to know. Or rather, they don't want to be reminded that they do know; for we all know everything; we have to know before deciding that we don't wish to know. We have to know that we don't want to know in order not to know. The censor knows what he is censoring. Every man is his own mesmerist.

We choose a level of ignorance in order to maintain a

balance. It is a question of priorities. In order to satisfy such needs as those for dependency, possessions, tyranny, sadism, emotional quietude, certain truths have to be concealed, and hypocrisies practised. To become aware of these ruses we play with ourselves is to have decided *already* not to play them any longer. We discover, because we know where to look.[6] When we are 'on to' a game we have been playing, we have already decided to play another.

But drugs like LSD can outwit us. They can thrust us into that part of ourselves that knows well the games and the stratagems we practise. The effect is then that we are 'on' to ourselves at the same time as we are still playing the game that we are pretending is not a game. The new lover has not arrived but we see that we no longer love the old. In between, then, we are faced with the prospect of having no lover, where that lover is, we fear, *ourselves*. How terrifying.

N. wanted reassurance from others who had experienced similar visions of reality to those she had had, and communication with persons familiar with LSD and its effects, both during the trip and afterwards, in various dimensions. She was able to get this.

For those who see through the delusions and hypocrisy of society,[7] of our socially conducted and constructed existences, there remain only two real alternatives : to hide their knowledge, or to find others who share it with whom to live and communicate.[8] There is a third alternative : to contain it, and preserve it, and use it purposefully to change others and the environment slowly and, as appropriate, towards honesty and flow (the Tao). But this is difficult to do, and work worthy of a Boddhisattva.[9]

Here are a few more letters.

[6] When we feel unready we 'fail' to find what others try to make us see in ourselves. This is 'resistance'.

[7] This awareness is probably the same as that of seeing through oneself (see above), but the awareness that they are the same is another awareness and has its own moment.

[8] For a fine fictional account of the existence and workings of this choice, see John Fowles, *The French Lieutenant's Woman*.

[9] In Mahayana Buddhism, a person who turns back on the threshold of *nirvana*, refusing to enter it until *all* sentient beings also attain it.

From Sheffield:

'. . . feel like I'm heading hard for the bin or the river, I need help – K.'

That's all. A white flag. A note in a bottle. Will anyone see it; find it? We did.

A letter from London:

'I've just read your thing in *IT*, I'm not anti-psychiatry and have no axe to grind in this direction but I've been in the bin a few times and know a bit how it feels. If I can help anyone who feels like this, I'll try – G.'

Not all who joined PNP were marching to war. This letter expresses simple human compassion.

From the Midlands:

'. . . for the last few years I've been quietly flipping and I've a feeling it might get worse. . . . I find it almost impossible to form lasting relationships with people because of my erratic mental state, mood swings. I've come to the conclusion that I need help. Ultimately only I can solve my own problems but I need some initial assistance. Assistance I've been unable to get so far. My doctor says, quote, "Pull yourself together. Here take these Valium tablets. You'll be alright." . . . Incidentally, I live with my parents and would not wish them to know of my contacting you. Actually I haven't communicated with them for some considerable time and keep my affairs much to myself.'

A case of delayed birth. Pregnant mothers have been known to hold on to their progeny for weeks beyond organically due date. People have been known to hold on to their own birth, as individuals, and as what they are, for the whole of their lives. When we cannot cut the cord we withdraw inside us from our parents and, to an extent, *from everyone else*.

A letter from Stan:

131

'. . . I seem to have lost myself somewhere, I'm hoping your thing might be of some kind of help.

'I don't seem to make it with people, but I'm so hung up with myself that there "doesn't seem to be much point to my existence", and other psychiatric clichés.

'Anyway, all I want is people, but I feel I'm invisible most of the time. I'm sick of feeling sorry for myself and stewing in my own isolation so I hope your lot can help, or help me to help myself.

With thanks & love. . . .'

Stan had withdrawn further and further from others, and the more he did so the less his basic needs for contact and communication with others were fulfilled, so that he felt worse, and less worthy, less alive, and therefore withdrew still further. Another vicious circle he was in was that at times his needs thrust forward and he became over-eager to make contact, indiscriminate, so that people felt assailed by him, and also not specifically themselves to him, but *anybody*. This made them wary and even hostile towards him, thereby reducing Stan's human contact still further. PNP, especially in some quarters, provided succour and hope to people like Stan because to a degree there was acceptance of others willy-nilly; you didn't have to be entertaining, or fascinating; you didn't have to prove anything.

At about this point in the first draft of this book I received this letter from Peter Wells, who was then right in the thick of PNP activity :

'There is a lot going on in PNP and people keep turning up and I think it's meaningful to them in the sense that *they can be sure of acceptance.*[10] It's like being turned on to life all the time.'

It was always beautiful to see the way lonely-looking and fearful people would come to PNP, to a small group or a large meeting, and then within about half an hour would be deep

[10] My italics.

132

in conversation, or some other form of communion, with other people. It was to watch suspended people come alive. Erving Goffman, the American sociologist, writes :

'. . . there seems to be no agent more effective than another person in bringing a world for oneself alive or, by a glance, a gesture, or a remark, shrivelling up the reality in which one is lodged.'[11]

What some can do to a person, perhaps others can undo. In a way, this was the central principle of PNP.[12]

Another letter – Jill from North London :

'I've read your articles in *IT* and am very interested in your movement for a new psychiatry. I'd like to join it and help in any way possible. I'd be very willing to listen to anyone who's hung up and needs someone to talk to, and I'd also like to come to the meetings, and to find out if you've any plans for setting up sanctuaries or anything for people who need them. I think it is a brilliant idea and I hope it will be success-ful.'

Not hard to see why I picked that one out for quote. Thank you Jill for your nice words and good wishes (again), and for containing in your short and simple letter the basic principles of anti-psychiatry.

This was Linda's letter. She was just sixteen, and came to PNP often :

'. . . . I think that what you have said is very true. I mean in particular that acceptance and understanding and honesty help very much to bring light to saddened people.

'I believe also, that finding peace within yourself will do more to alleviate a "stewed up frame of mind" than any anti-depression pill will do, in the long run, that is.

'But unfortunately, I don't speak as one who has found this peace. I have had fleeting glimpses of it and I've been

---

[11] In *Encounters*.
[12] See author's *New Society* article.

nearer the brink of hell than I am at the moment, but inwardly I'm alone with it all in spite of the people about me.

'Studying Zen and other sections of Buddhism has helped me a lot though.

'As individuals maybe we have to tread our own paths, but we can try to help each other along the way.

'I feel in need of help, but I think that this would come by being able to help others, if I could, and I do so want to.

I feel a fool writing all this, but I mean it all sincerely,

Love & Peace.'

To Linda, the basic flaw in chemotherapy was obvious. On the other hand, to many brilliant scientific minds it is not obvious. To me it is obvious; but what is obvious to us may be just what prevents us from seeing. What is obvious tends not to be questioned. For instance, it is obvious that the sun moves round the earth, but it does not. To some people blacks are obviously inferior to whites, to others it is obvious that we need motorways even if our countryside has to be destroyed. In short, nothing is certain, however obvious. Nevertheless it remains obvious to me that drugs cure nothing.[13] At best they smooth over. Or at worst; for they may hide an increasing devastation. A latent conflict is that degree more dangerous than a patent one, for we cannot trace its progress until, perhaps, it is too late. I suspect that there is a direct relationship between the use of psychiatric drugs and the increased incidence of cancer. Symptoms can be healthy, for they express conflict in a safe way. They are both a statement and a release mechanism. Smother them and the conflict will find a more drastic way of expressing itself – a fresh growth to live for the repressed and rejected parts of the organism, a growth which once started cannot be stopped, and goes into a death cycle.

The biggest problem facing the psychiatrists with their new 'anti-schizophrenic' drug fluphenazine is, they say, the tendency of patients to cease taking the drug when they improve.

[13] On the other hand I have become aware that drugs can allay desperate situations, bring a patient to a point where real work with him can be done.

This apparently is disastrous. What is the difference between this and addiction?

Finally a letter from W. in Hertfordshire :

'This idea of yours, it sounds great. I think most people think of this but never try it. The environment I'm in is a fairly cool town, but we feel it should be better to live and be in. . . . If everyone knew each other and were friends or just friendly it would be great. If any friends would like to come down for weekends I should think we could put them up, not too many you know. There's sounds to listen to, a park just outside with deer, and things for play. . . .

'Hope this idea of yours can be brought across in a big way. Love. . . .'

It may seem incredible that such simplicity and human warmth could have anything to do with psychiatry, with its wards and hospitals, its white coats and busy staff, its drugs, its ECT and its solemn brain surgery. It depends on whether you see psycho-pathology as minds in need of mechanistic correction, or as sickness of the soul; it depends whether you see cure and heal-ing in terms of science or in terms of human beings and the ways they relate. Naturally it is not one or the other, for most people would accept the usefulness of both. But it does depend where your emphasis is, and today, psychiatry rests far too close to the pure pole of dehumanized science.

Here, and in the last chapter, I have drawn up some of the revolutionary army. It was amazing that later it was to give parts of the garrison the jitters.

Stone

Paranoia is the phantasy of being threatened or under attack.[1] It results from the projection of personal conflicts. Usually, the paranoiac identifies with one side in the conflict and projects the other side into the world or on to specific others. Where an entire group indulges itself in this gambit these others become outcasts, scapegoats, enemies or, some claim, the mentally ill.

PNP began to receive such projection from parts of the establishment. Anyone who accepts more or less in its entirety a systemized mode of thought or functioning, which is learned rather than evolved out of personal experience, is sure to be in conflict, even without knowing it. We cannot be given ways of seeing the world like this; every perspective is unique. Therefore when we are hostile to those who oppose a way of life or a mode of operation that we have adopted it is because they express our own doubts and uncertainties. If we were sure in ourselves, we would be able to ignore the objectors and the sceptics.

Commitment, therefore, is a dangerous thing. I identify with a cause, a religion, an ideology; then when it is under attack so I feel am I. If I am tied to something, a belief, an idea, then I am no longer free. What I have attached myself to must be seen therefore as worthy of my sacrifice. It must not be scorned, belittled, faulted, for to reduce its value is to diminish my sacrifice; that is, to diminish me.

The orthodox always risk falling into this trap, and thereby losing themselves, their creativity and freshness. They then

[1] For an interesting view that paranoia in our society is not phantasy but real, not sick but healthy, in fact 'the beginning of active existence', see Cooper, *Death of the Family*.

react to challenge fixedly, with chapter and verse, and even paranoia, rather than with openness, flexibility and flow.

The extent of professional jealousy and fear behind the urbanity and the intellectual wisdom is often intense.

Take the case of Brian P.

Brian was a sociologist working in a certain famous London hospital. He felt the personal approach to psychiatric patients was severely lacking and so he began trying out a healing method based chiefly on warmth, interest and concern, with one or two. There was opposition, but Brian persevered.

He was a friend of David Eddy's and at David's suggestion Brian began to come to the PNP open meetings – which were held every Friday, and were attended by anything between twenty and a hundred PNP members. Brian was very enthusiastic. He thought these meetings, especially when they were smaller, would be an excellent setting in which labelled and depersonalized patients could regain their sense of worth. For at these meetings like everyone else they would be treated simply as people. Brian put this messianic idea to the hospital authorities, who refused at once to sanction it. However he did receive permission to arrange a talk on PNP to members of staff – and that was quite a breakthrough.

David Eddy and I were asked along. There was a gathering of twenty-five or so administrators, matrons, registrars, training psychiatrists; no consultants. The reaction to our description of PNP in principle and in action was, on the whole, ferocious, beneath a thin layer of courtesy. We were told we were interfering where we had no business to. Mental illness belonged to psychiatry, since psychiatry was there to deal with mental illness – an argument that is merely circular. The antagonism of the women present was particularly excessive. I had the feeling that this was partly due to the fact that they were struggling furiously to make it in what was still largely a man's world, psychiatry, and David and I were suggesting that the prize was a monkey trick. Some left in a huff, others gnashing their teeth. A small group decided that, with vetting, we might possibly be of use as a kind of after-sales service, in view of hospital pressure; perhaps we could relieve them of this work. Classic assimilation technique. Others tried to simply annihilate us in discussion. But, having nothing to lose, and not petitioning for gain, David and I could stay cool.

Then a quiet man, a registrar, stood up and spoke, saying something like this :

'It is time we faced up to the fact that we are working very much in the dark. People come to this hospital in various states of distress, and we try out the limited methods we have at our disposal. We all well know that sometimes none of them work. Our choice is narrow, and our time short. We get very little time to get to know our patients at all as people, and I have always felt very unhappy about this. Now we have two visitors who have told us that in their experience much can be done for distressed persons by means of the basic principles of human relationship. Through acceptance, care and confirmation. I think that it is time that we in this hospital, like them, moved away from our clever methods, which so often seem to miss the mark, towards the simplicity of human warmth and care.'

In the silence that followed you could hear the knives being sharpened. Eventually others spoke as if nothing had been said. A group of registrars became politely violent in their defence of ECT, which both David and I had attacked. They insisted that it was benevolent, and it came down to their refusal to give a status to PNP unless we accepted in principle the use of ECT. This we refused to do. The meeting dribbled away into the sand, to be forgotten after the next tide.

But not quite. Before very long both Brian P. and the registrar had lost their jobs.

Before this happened Brian did manage to arrange for one patient he had been working with, George, to come to a PNP meeting – but accompanied by a nurse, which of course almost wholly wiped out the possibilities of benefit to George. Out on parole, he was handcuffed to a gaoler.

Many consider that, up to a point, people are 'mentally ill' because they want to be. I do not quite go along with this. What happens rather is that certain human beings, as a result

138

of early experiences (or *karma*, if you like), become afflicted with 'growth disorders',[2] or neuroses. Naturally they attempt to make the best of their situation by using these neuroses, manifested as fixed structures in a world of flux, to fulfil needs and gain satisfactions – which are often masochistic. The move from neurosis to health involves the surrendering of these surrogate and second-class satisfactions for the chance of others that will far outshine them.[3] This is the neurotic's dilemma. Giving up what he has got may lead him to nothingness, or to the treasure of a real self. Getting well involves taking this gamble *over and over again*.

I have experienced this dilemma recently in the game of tennis. For twenty-five years I have played tennis 'neurotically' – wrong grip, wrong stance, wrong movements, wrong strokes. A few weeks ago I began taking lessons for the first time in my life. *Everything has to go*, in particular my belief that I must get the ball over the net and into the other court *at any price*. I have to literally start again. The *correct* hold I experience as a *distortion*, so long have I held the racquet improperly. Holding it correctly I experience as *pain*. For a while it was very hard to accept that it was better for me to move and strike properly and miss, and even look foolish, than to get the ball back, even as a winner, using my old ways. There was a time, though it did not last long, when I wanted to *cry* for my old game, for its ease and comfort. But already, after six lessons, I am playing tennis better than ever before, and with much more satisfaction.[4]

I believe abandoning a neurosis is much like this, except that the game is life, and it is played every minute of every day.

[2] The term is Fritz Perls'.

[3] J. N. Rosen writes: 'It is only after the psychotic has discovered a full measure of the happiness of maturity that he is no longer interested in or concerned with the phoney values of the psychosis.' See *Direct Analysis*.

[4] 'There was a crooked man who walked a crooked mile' – and probably walking crookedly 'felt right' to him. As F. M. Alexander, the creator of the Alexander technique, would point out, bad habits often 'feel right', and more efficient and co-ordinated ways of doing things can 'feel wrong', at least for a while. See, for example, F. M. Alexander: *The Resurrection of the Body*.

This is the letting go, the finding of that nothingness in which infinity is.

We are all patients to the extent that we cling on to ourselves – as something fixed, with habits, fixations, character and permanence. Those of us who do this most are *called* patients, or the mentally ill. And as patients cling on to their neuroses, their fixed patterns, so psychiatrists cling on to *them*.

Therapists cling on to their patients, as patients, often unwittingly. The sick play helpless and won't let go of their helpers, who in turn are loth to let go of them. There is collusion. The situation is nicely stabilized. You play patient and I'll play doctor. Children do it. But with adults, it is no game, or at least no joke, because it goes on into life. Roles freeze and the situation gets nailed to the ground. Everyone is happy, for they escape the flow, and forget that they are free.[5]

Anti-psychiatry expresses, amongst other things, the wish of many to break out of the prison of their set of roles. Encounter groups, the whole Human Potential movement, PNP – all these attempt to provide settings in which people can take risks and experiment with their freedom.

This freedom resides in the body and in feelings. It also exists in the mind – but only when it is clear and open. Thought, thought about things, facts : these tie. 'Pure intelligence is . . . a product of dying . . . and is therefore in principle madness' (Ferenczi). All values are body values. *Cut off from the body and the feelings, the life of the mind is meaningless.*

The avowed goal of psychoanalysis is to make the unconscious conscious. There is an extent to which there must also be a flow the other way – from conscious control, judgement and analysis, to natural instinctual flow.

This is not the same thing as chaos, barbarism, irrationality. In a way there has to be a journey into the ego consciousness – and back. From instinct to consciousness, and then to what Nietzsche called 'the transfigured *physis*'. This famous Zen saying expresses the same thing :

[5] This collusion of 'winner' and 'loser' is evoked powerfully by Genet in *The Balcony*.

At first the mountains are mountains;
Next the mountains are no longer mountains;
Finally the mountains are once again mountains.

I believe Samuel Butler was getting at the same thing when he wrote, nearly a hundred years ago :

'You are stirring mud . . . or poking at a sleeping dog. You are trying to make people resume consciousness about things, which, with sensible men, have already passed into the unconscious stage. The men whom you would disturb are in front of you, and not, as you fancy, behind you; it is you who are the lagger, not they.'[6]

Or, more recently, Laing, saying in effect the same thing :

'True sanity entails in one way or another the dissolution of the normal ego, that false self competently adjusted to our alienated social reality; the emergence of the "inner" archetypal mediators of divine power, and through this death a rebirth, and the eventual re-establishment of a new kind of ego-functioning, the ego now being the servant of the divine, no longer its betrayer.'[7]

But back to establishment paranoia again. I was asked, early in 1971, to give a talk on PNP at a synagogue. Present were some two hundred people, including doctors, dentists, chemists, psychiatrists. When the talk was over I was attacked violently. Certain members of the audience were outraged. How dare we do what we were doing? It was gross interference; dangerous amateurism. If a car goes wrong, you take it to a garage. If a mind goes haywire, you take it to a psychiatrist. It was so obvious. But not to me, which was unforgivable. In another age I would have been stoned, at least. Fortunately I was, but in a different way. The violence seething in the hall reached a peak – on the question of violence. What did

[6] From *The Way of all Flesh*.
[7] From *The Politics of Experience*.

we do if someone became violent? I said that out of thousands, nobody ever had. *But what if they did?* I couldn't say. My actions would depend on the immediate situation. I was accused of being evasive, of being irresponsible. Voices were raised, fists were flourished, someone was talking and spitting with rage. A riot rumbled – almost broke. Stoned, I let it all run over me, so much so that I couldn't muster the purpose to answer their accusations. This must have been very provoking. Fortunately I had roused a group of supporters in the audience who were dealing with the opposition far more ably than I could. One said, 'It is clear from what Mr Barnett has told us that people who go to PNP do not manifest violence because nothing about the way those in it conduct themselves and treat their contacts triggers it off. On the other hand, from what I know of psychiatrists and mental hospitals, the reverse is often the case. They way patients are treated is quite sufficient sometimes, I would have thought, to provoke the very violence which the experts then proceed to diagnose and contain.' I had a real ball, sitting up there on the dais, listening to others putting my arguments so well and so coolly, whilst the opposition expressed so clearly through their own behaviour where the violence they were afraid for really lay. Gradually the meeting polarized – for and against; some people actually crossed the gangway, like politicians changing parties. I was ignored, forgotten, which, high as I was, felt fine. It ended, with tempers still frayed. A small group escorted me out, through the scrums and the cold shoulders.

Psychiatric approaches to persons are, then, often capable of producing violence. Moreover, its attitude to it, once it appears, lacks imagination.

Here is Bill Schutz, Encounter leader, Ph.D. in psychology, ex-lecturer at Harvard and at Berkeley, comparing, from experience, the attitudes of orthodox psychiatry and the Human Potential movement, to violence (or the explosion of suppressed anger):

'When I was working at the Albert Einstein School of Medicine in New York, a thoroughly respectable institution, I learned

142

what to do with patients who freak out. Once a patient started acting crazy. He was immediately surrounded by three attendants, his arms were pinned back, and he was given a shot of tranquillizer, a standard procedure that seemed to me at the time very sensible. Shortly after I arrived at Esalen,[8] a similar experience occurred. During an evening drum dance, a girl freaked out. She started screaming uncontrollably, threw herself on to the middle of the dance floor, and started pounding her fists into the floor. I could feel my reflexes starting to operate as I started to run toward her to grab her and somehow tranquillize her. After all, I certainly knew how to handle these matters more than the Big Sur mountain people. Before I could reach her, two of the Big Sur women were on the floor next to her, soothing her brow. One of the Big Sur drummers, Ron, was saying, "Let there be no fear on this floor," and kept drumming while the Big Sur women kept soothing. No one attempted to stop her, "She's doing her thing," they later explained, "that's what she has to do now. We're here, available if she needs us." Then Ron shouted out, "I'll be here thirty days and thirty nights if you need me," and the beat went on. People danced around her. Finally she stopped, and very shaken, started to walk over to a table, accompanied by the girls. She sat down and began a long process of collecting herself.'[9]

Here is Schutz's comment on the happening:

'I was very taken with this whole scene, and very impressed. The Big Sur community assumed that she was doing what she needed to do, no condescension, no infantalizing; simply, here is a girl whose life state requires her to freak out right now. She is responsible for her psychotic episode, she is choosing to do it. We choose to help her through it, with a very supportive attitude giving her acceptance and respect. Since that incident, I have become more familiar with the work of Laing with schizophrenics and others who regard psychosis as often a good

[8] Esalen Institute, California: the place where the whole Encounter movement started.
[9] From *Here Comes Everybody*.

thing, a positive disintegration, and I have had personal experiences leading me to believe that the assumption that a person is choosing to go crazy, and that he can within wide limits determine his own behaviour, is both accurate and very helpful for encouraging the person to use his greatest abilities.'[10]

Anyone who has been to even a few Encounter groups will have seen people do things that done elsewhere would lead to hospitalization on the grounds, specific diagnosis apart, that such persons were dangerous to themselves and others. Yet, for all the freaking and the acting out and the explosive confrontations, I have never seen anyone get injured, beyond a scuff or a bruise. And, through expression of deep-seated and long-suppressed emotions I have seen people move into a new calmness and stillness, seen them become free of tensions for a while, tensions due to the restraint and the control, and I have sensed in them a new freedom as a result of relieving themselves of this mammoth task of clamping themselves down. There is no magic here, no instant enlightenment or miraculous cures. It takes a lot of work, both in and outside the groups, before old patterns of control and inhibition are broken. But it can be done, and done, I believe, far more effectively, more *integrally*, and more quickly than through the orthodox methods of psychotherapy.

Though we had no violence in PNP, we did have freak-outs, that is explosions of emotion, or overflows, not directed at a particular person, but just moving out of an individual who was unable, or who was refusing, to hold on to it any longer. It was handled much as the Big Sur people handled it: as part of the person's flow of life, as something to be gone through, not blocked, stultified, diagnosed or indicted. At times it could last for hours, such a freak-out, but if you believed in your heart that it was good and necessary, there was little difficulty in allowing it to roll along on its way.

Life is flow. So are these attitudes to turbulent emotional behaviour. Much of society is control and stasis. So are the attitudes of conventional psychiatry.

[10] *Ibid.*

Hips

There was nothing more to be done, once PNP was there, but allow it to grow. The word spread : PNP existed. It was not a myth, but people who would see you, listen, be with you. It was alive and real, and to be had. Several other networks began very soon in the provinces. Leeds was the first, set up by Ted Brown. It has lasted, others taking it on after Ted. The London network grew fast. People, hearing about it, came to see for themselves – and stayed to become part of it.

The infrastructure, the list of core members, grew too. Bill Young joined. Bill shared a flat with Mike Williamson. He too dropped out of advertising and took the various trips that Mike did. But he came out in a different place – with his feet well on the ground. He gave of himself in PNP, yet stayed in himself. There was nothing in him that needed those who came, as there was in some of us, like me, like Mike.

John O'Shea, fellow of mystery and pain, held on to himself, but gave of space and time, and a perfect fun. David and Cathy Neilson offered themselves and their home as openly as could be, until their callers seemed to me to become invaders, staying for days or even weeks. Perhaps they found it hard to allow themselves to say No – something you had to learn if you were not to get sucked under. There was a time to say No. Without it the work could become exhausting and a terrible chore. There was a time to call Enough, if you were not to risk ending up hating all comers. But perhaps I am talking not about David and Cathy, but about me.

It seems to me we are always likely to end up hating those to whom we give over-generously. For instance, it is a common experience to hate the one to whom we have confessed, in a lax moment, a guarded secret. We need to find out how to

K

give to and grow from our own selves. Taking the line of least resistance (due to laziness, cowardice, fear) towards others, rather than the stiff steep path to ourselves, makes us feel unworthy of ourselves – and then we take our resentment out on others.[1]

Part of the problem was that PNP was *in opposition*. The Encounter movement was not; it had sprung up to express a new ethos, an alternative set of values. It was not always easy to say what you felt in PNP, for there was an overt intent to offset the insensitivity and callousness of orthodox psychiatry[2] – which led to a feeling that niceness and kindness were always appropriate for those who were suffering. This was the outcome of linear thinking : if not callousness, then kindness.

But another, and richer, alternative to treating others impersonally is to be straight and honest with them, for these *affirm*.

There is no other way to find out about one another other than through honesty of expression and equivalence of word and feeling.

If we fail to find out about one another there can never be peace for peace is based on acceptance, not on appeasement and self-control, still less on indifference.

Nevertheless honesty grew in PNP as we became less idealistic and learned from our mistakes.

For some, dependence is a way of life. There were those who came to hand themselves over to us. It could be a soft trap. Someone plays helpless in an area that is effortless for you. So you do something for them. They are grateful, they praise you. Can you do this too? they want to know. You show you can, and in no time you are hooked. You become the other's pawn. Though you are the actor, the other is in control, because he has decreed that you should act for him. Neurotics are experts at this meta-control.

Jack Lewis joined up with us, though part of the orthodox

[1] 'Whoever is dissatisfied with himself is always ready to revenge himself therefor : we others will be his victims.' Nietzsche, *The Gay Science*.

[2] A friend of mine, an art therapist, was hauled before a board at a psychiatric hospital because she was discovered with her arm comfortingly around a female patient. She was accused of having an unhealthy attitude towards patients.

brigade – he worked at the Tavistock. He was more political than most of us, like Jenny was, but no matter. Nothing like this mattered since we had no set scene. People in PNP were free to be as they were entirely. No one spoke for PNP. No one could since it had no existence. Only its members did.

Others joined, and gave much, like Tony and Margaret Grace, to visit whom was a treat, for they offered total attention and concern; David Martin, who couldn't do enough; Terry, a Ph.D., whose mind was a beautiful creation.

We would meet quite often, this infrastructure, in small groups, sometimes as a whole. Then the meetings were thrown open. Once a week there was a place where anyone in PNP could go, and meet others. Numbers increased, once grew to a hundred. Flats groaned as people crammed in. Nothing much seemed to be happening, yet people came back and back. It was something to do with acceptance and with respect. These just seemed to be there for whoever came.

There were always new people, looking for PNP, and staying to become part of it. Some left disappointed, without solutions. Others found important relationships that continued apart from PNP. It was a loose network of people moving together towards something – perhaps independence : from the family, and from a patterned society; and helping one another to stay out of trouble through the upheaval that inevitably accompanies this development to self-centring and personal integrity.

That is how I saw it. But there never was an official agreed statement about the purpose and meaning of PNP. We shared a number of each, and none of them jarred. There were no fights on principles and policy since anything was allowed. The association between us all was, in a sense, instinctive. Since that was there, we could trust one another and lose no sleep.

It might be timely here to give other slants on PNP. At the end of November 1969, *IT* gave a double-page spread to PNP under the heading 'Psychiatry and Consciousness'. It consisted of seven letters written by different members of PNP –

not all list-members; each gives a unique point of view, a separate personal experience of PNP. Here are some letters, and others extracts.

Firstly, Pam Barnett's letter :

'People ring up. I don't know them, but in a sense they know me, or Mike, or whoever answers the phone, because they've heard of the network. I think there is trust because of what they've read of the PNP letters and articles in *IT*. I mean about the acceptance, non-judgement, non-role-playing etc. The conversation may last a minute or an hour. On the face of it, making a phone call, perhaps the only one, is nothing much. We can't say what emerges from it. We can't put a finger on it and say, "Aha, now, there's an example of PNP in action. This happened or that happened." Nothing cut and dried like that. Out of ten calls there is an immediate follow-up of about half, maybe less. But on each occasion someone took a step – maybe a long one for them, in an attempt to make contact. AND THERE WAS SOMEONE THERE TO ANSWER IT. I think this is important. The knowledge that there is some other source beyond the ones you've tried (you can go round in circles on your own and often friend/relationships are too closed or ground into a particular groove to help very much) is so reassuring that this alone is a terrific relief. We get lots of phone calls. We are a link. What in or of I'm not sure; in communication? In recognition of another's existence? It might be anything. What at the time may be a fringe hang-up, might very easily become a specific one if there is no outlet.

'What else do we do? Examples :

'(1) A girl rings up. She is feeling frightened because of her sense of aloneness. She wants to come and see us. It's 1.30 a.m. and at 2.00 a.m. she arrives very frightened, in tears. She talks for a long time, we all talk. And then no talking, just drinking our coffee and being at ease, and then she's so relaxed it's lovely. And then we all start laughing because 3.00 a.m. is a good time to be laughing. She knows she can kip down for the night if she wants, but she's happy to leave because the blackness has gone. Being alone is one thing; but to feel you're the only one is terrifying.

'(2) J. has done the rounds, this therapist, that one. J. is so lonely that one hour a week with a time-conscious, very busy guy is not enough. He sees several people on the network regularly, stays a few hours, listens to music, leaves. Sometimes he talks, sometimes says nothing, just plays with the baby or has a bath. Inter-relation is not such a toil as it was. He knows there are no rigid time limits, no strict formalities to observe. (I can't say that his hang-ups are all gone, he's just coping a lot better than he was.)

'People write long letters. They say it's a relief to write to someone. We write back. Another link is made. Some just drop in. It's a bit chancy. We might not be there or whatever. If it's OK they stay. It usually is, but if not they get a list of the network, can call someone and go on to their place if they want.

'The essence of PNP travels by word of mouth. The more distant contacts are forming their own PNP amidst their own environment. Each network is bound to be different; there is no central group to deal out instructions or ideologies, though there's an intercom of experience, exchange of ideas, etc. Anyway I feel it's working for a lot of people. It's working for me.'

Here is the essence of PNP, found in the words laid on a page by someone who experienced it from the beginning. In a way, no more than this needs to be said, except that there are other angles. Where else could you go if you wanted to share your state with someone who was not a professional, not a relative or a friend? There are other organizations like the Samaritans, there for the desperate, but these belong to ways of centring that are of social value, rather than to centring in the self. This was why to some PNP appealed. No lessons would be offered, no bedtime stories, no social collusions. You would have to face yourself and find out who you were, even if it was not pretty.

Now, a letter from Ian Spooner, an architectural student at the college where David Eddy taught:

149

'PNP is an alternative to psychiatric treatment when the tension becomes too much, when you find yourself at a dead end and need to communicate with others who have been through or are going through the same things. People need people; we are all moving somewhere, developing through our contacts with others, finding out about life and how we relate to it; we need you as much as you may need us at the times when you feel yourself alone.

'It is difficult, I know, to make contact with the unknown, difficult to admit to yourself that you need help, to pick up the phone and speak to a stranger about yourself. I was lucky in meeting David Eddy because I would probably never have made the phone call; even though I had read the articles in *IT* about alternatives to psychiatry and knew that I must become involved in order to preserve other people and probably myself at some time, from the fate of friends who had been "cured". They have returned grey ciphers, their sense of love and beauty destroyed and their minds blank; which isn't surprising after electric shock treatment, degradation and the regendering of the guilt syndrome which we have to eradicate as first step in the discovery of life.

'There is always an alternative; we can choose our path at any moment of life, that's one of its excitements. Remember PNP is there if you need people.'

Next, here comes Jenny James :

'PNP is a disaster. It's the admittance that there's so few people left, they've got to be found, artificially collated. And most of your energy goes in trying to re-awaken in the folks who think they're OK, the idea that keys can be used to open doors as well as to lock them. . . .

'I'm with PNP for hate's sake : I want to smile the doctor's vested interest in unhappiness out of existence. I relish a vision : men in white coats crisply marching, eternally puzzled, up and down sterile empty wards, ignored, redundant.

'PNP is a disease, sadly not too virulent, but let's hope its infection spreads and reaches plague proportions. When the

150

sad ones use the energy of their sadness to happify the even sadder, then the thing's working. PNP's worked for me : I've found at last some folks you can be with unstiffly without fear of that "Oh-my-god" reaction.'

Another perspective, quite cosmic, came from Terry :

'Our technological environment has offered us a falsely sub-stantive view of the world. Periodically some of the bastions of science are attacked. Godel has printed out the incon-sistencies in mathematics, neo-Darwinism has failed to explain species adaptation by random genetic mutations. Every one of our technological advances has an unpleasant kickback, e.g. cyclamates, DDT, atmospheric and river pollution etc. Is our Technic applied logically? Or do we suffer from techno-irrationality? . . .

'Let us start again from the beginning, with people not simply reflex arcs, communication not alienation is our aim. Let us abandon cosy notions of conspiracy in high places to preserve the status quo. Apathy and failure to communicate preserves the system, nothing else.

'Let us therefore manipulate the system, not be manipulated by it.'

Graham Spowatt whizzed around the network like a seasoned rocket, whirling in, bursting out, to return, aflame with energy. He wrote his views somewhere in orbit; an extract :

'The people who meet are not in any specific clinic to be cured, confronted by the psychiatrist who embodies a lost normality which they will eventually attain after treatment. Those in the network meet each other as friends who went to see each other voluntarily to communicate in any way without a physical and interpersonal situation which reinforces the feeling that one is to be cured.

'I do not by any means contest the help which individual psychiatrists may have succeeded in giving to certain people,

151

but it may well be that psychiatry has taken over large areas of human behaviour and experience which it in fact aggravates by the clinical and medical aura which surrounds it.'

Orthodox psychiatry concerns itself with adjustment. It has, despite denials, the goal of readjusting those who do not fit, so that they will. It represents society in defence of its frontiers.[3] It leans on society for its values. To this extent it distances itself from universal man, that is from the ultimate in the individual. The Humanistic Psychology movement, of which PNP is a natural part, is concerned not with the adaptation of men and women to a principally rigid system, but with the growth of human beings *continuously*, the release and realization of more and more potential. This will take them beyond the needs and requirements of their social existences, resulting, ultimately, in the formation of a different kind of society based on their higher values.

Except that 'movement' is a dubious word, finding itself too often in association with such others as ideology, dogma, commitment, aims. I like to think PNP's expression of people's desires and wants has none of these. What would be welcome is not a new line in living and being together, but no line at all, but an exponential relational curve based on experience. This kind of thing :

'The following word offering about PNP represents an opinion at the moment of writing and like all opinions merits quick listening and quick forgetting : the thing itself, in this case PNP, continues as ungraspably as before.

'For those who didn't know, PNP is an almost unestablished diffuse kind of network thing about as vague or defined as you or I, at whose conversation tables anyone suffering from acute personism or individualitis or whatever is welcome to play. Each of us here at PNP and elsewhere is a qualified, practising human with an average of ninety-eight degrees odd.

'Person please don't fight your environment or yourself. Let

[3] This is accepted by even such a conservative sociologist as Talcott Parsons. See, for example, his *Social Structure and Personality*.

us sit down and talk about each and all, who under the surface may not be different. On the surface there seems to be little else but differences (another word for strife), which may range from trifling annoyances and generally shitty feelings to the agonies of acute personism or individualitis, where you seem to be sealed off from life and others in a whirling capsule of pain and confusion. When in this condition, stop, loosen tensed muscles, go limp, alight alertly at PNP.

'PNP means us and where we can talk together in peace and we hope understanding, beginning an association perhaps from scratch then scratch will maybe turn out to be a unique movement or a kind of song and not a wound. As to the so-called games of role playing, protest, success, politics, achievement, business, life insurance, identity, jobupmanship, estate management, education and so on, it seems to me that we hope for only minor variations, based as these are on the themes of fear, greed, envy, and the other central motifs of the I-experience. As games, they are a very poor effort indeed; they are "played" in deadly cut-throat seriousness and you had better do well, follow the rules etc., or you'll be a failure, and the rules say you have to play at least one of the authorized games, like it or no. You must be very serious indeed, but should also be happy and optimistic and enjoy even the most brutally boring routine. To worry yourself to death about your performance in life is quite normal so – as Bristow might say – not to worry! Every now and then the general frustration and boredom rises to a deafening crescendo and war and famine carry off a large number of the "players". Like "players", "game" gets battered out of all recognition as such. If you come to PNP (and please do) you won't have to play any games if you don't want to. Piece.'

So wrote John O'Shea for those *IT* pages. John often saw like a beam of white light. He could climb to where he could see what was happening panoramically. It may be that he cut down the pain of this vision by cutting himself out, as part of it. Minimizing his personal reality he was able to grasp the general. Many of us, his friends, were grateful for that.

Freud, it has been said, invented psychoanalysis for him-self – it was the therapy he needed. Fritz Perls was anxious to mend his own fragmentation, so, being a genius, he invented his own method – Gestalt Therapy.[4]

No doubt PNP was intended to be my own insurance, apart from meeting my immediate needs. Distrusting all systematic psychiatry, all orthodoxy, I probably hoped that people would stand me in good stead, and even cure me, when I broke down, as I'm sure I expected to do soon, back in 1969.

But when it happened I found I had no heart to use it, this network of beautiful people. I could not use my own creation. I stayed alone. Nothing would induce me to offer myself to those I had chosen to surround me for just, let us conjecture, such an eventuality. One way or the other, I failed myself.

September 1969. I was accepted by Birmingham University to do a Master's degree in Sociology. I wanted this, feeling myself over-orientated towards the individual, largely ignorant of the social pressures at work. How right was Marx? Did social class really determine all? Was my whole psychology, not to mention my life, the product of my social situation since birth? I could not believe it, yet to an extent it might be true. How far then must I modify the atomic innocence of my vision of man?

My marriage was making me uneasy at the time. I was beginning to feel restless. I felt I no longer wished to be tied or exclusive, as I had allowed myself to be in my relationship with Pamela. I told her, on leaving, that I wasn't sure when or if I would be back. Part of me was definitely moving base. The rest wasn't, and wanted to leave open the door. This put the screws on Pam.

But she shook them off. Under the helplessness, in crises, she was a tough cookie. She has a kernel that is indomitable, this woman, and I see it time and again, when it comes to the crunch, *beyond* the crunch.

When I returned home on a visit after about six weeks Pam had begun setting something up with X, a PNP member. After the initial shock – for in five and a half years neither of us

[4] An opinion shared by Perls' close friend Marty Fromm.

had slept with another – I found I could accept the sexual performance. After all I had egged her on often enough. I suppose there was jealousy, but I fed this with elaborate confession elicited from her. Also there was the question of my own unadmitted homosexual feelings toward X. This made it all a bit exciting.

But then the involvement between them became emotional. This was another pair of shoes. I was shattered. I couldn't stay in Birmingham without being seized by the need to speed pell mell for London. When I did Pam was always out, the flat empty. She would be over at the flat with X and his friends. For a while I struggled manfully (?) to accept it, to permit her her freedom. Her freedom? Her self. But I failed. The war went on. She was living my beliefs but I was far from feeling them. What I did feel, however, I denied. Of course I didn't feel – lost? abandoned? excluded? betrayed? – no, impossible, I am all for it, for Pam doing her thing, said my head. The tension became intolerable. I moved back to London. Jenny James, who had moved in with Pam with her daughter Becky, moved out. Finally I collapsed.

I begged Pam to cut off from X for a while. I hated myself. How could I do it? But I did. Of course I stopped nothing that mattered. Other people's emotions, sadly, were out of my control. But Pam did cut off from X physically. I actually sent her round to see him to tell him she wouldn't be seeing him for a while. She made the sacrifice. I got my respite.

But I saw that I had achieved nothing. I could not make her stay with me, whole, this way. Emotionally, part of her was elsewhere, and that was that. Finally I was forced to face facts. I saw my dependence that had been behind, for years, Pam's apparent dependence on me. It was I who was the child, not her. This realization was ghastly. My state – of collapse – was hard to bear. The *fact* that I was in such a state was even harder to accept. It was indefensible, grotesque. Yet so.

For a while I was like jelly. Surrounded by people, in the midst still of PNP, I could bear no one. Except David Eddy. He came one day and bore my sobs. Then he said he understood. It was the fact that the affair had been with X that was the trouble. If it had been him, David, I would surely have not minded. This was so far from the truth, I choked. At once I sobered up. From then on I was alone. Except for Pam, who could do nothing without betraying herself. And should she do this, I would know, and hate her for that too. Yet, like Telephus,[5] I felt only she could cure me. Later I saw that no one could cure me. Cure could come only through letting go, and time.[6]

So I let go, and gradually I mended. I fought myself out of the squelch of a shared existence, as I had never done from my mother as a child.[7] I wrestled my way at last into my own air. I was able to stand on my own feet without swaying as, unknowingly, I always had before. I could look at the world, begin to really experience it, without falling into it. Finally I was able to leave Pam, allow her to leave me, to separate, and subsequently feel the freedom throughout me that once, Birmingham bound, had not reached beyond my desires and the thoughts in my head.[8]

[5] Telephus, injured by a spear, could be healed only by the touch of the injuring weapon.

[6] 'I have never known one person who did not fully go into their particular madness and come out of it within about ten days given a certain lack of interference in the guise of treatment.' David Cooper, *Death of the Family*.

[7] 'If one does not discover one's autonomy in one's first years of life and if one does not discover it by this anguished moment in later childhood, one is either driven mad in late adolescence, or one gives up the ghost and becomes a normal citizen, or one battles one's way through to a freedom in the working-out of subsequent relationships.' *Ibid.*

[8] In fact, I was never quite alone. Always there was Shem, my small son, in support.

Haws

No hierarchy. That was important to the spirit of PNP. We were all equal – just people. But saying so is to avoid the extent to which all of us are less than we are. Essence and existence are different. Equality may be a reality at the essential level. We all have an *atman*. But existentially it depends on disorders, distortions, plus the plane upon which persons are operating. Equality as an idea is, in most situations, crippling and imprisoning. It is to confuse the ultimate with the temporal, to ignore dormancy and destruction. It is to equate the Zen master with the Fascist brute.

We all have holes.[1] We discover other people who seem full where we seem empty, who function in ways we do not. Through contact with them we hope to utilize their specific power, or mobilize that power in ourselves. This is often at the root of therapy.

Once, the person I was having therapy with was in love with a person who was having therapy with me. We all have our holes. And how to sort that one out hierarchically?

Did those on the network list constitute an elite? An 'Us' to their visitors' 'Them'? What was my position in October 1969? Before my departure for Birmingham the infrastructure had a meeting to decide what would happen in my absence. In principle nothing need be done, for I was just one of many. I said so. But it was obviously absurd, in practice. The decision was unanimous that I should need to be replaced. A group of five was elected: Mike, Bill Young, David, Frank McAllan and Pam. Five for me. The number seemed about right.

Jenny James moved in with Pam and began to spread her straw socialism over the network. With a sharpish knife of

[1] See Perls, *Gestalt Therapy Verbatim*, especially p. 39ff.

157

course. Jenny would not abide a whiff of Them and Us, though in practice, like the rest of us, she was full of distinctions : the over-thirties/the under-thirties; straights and freaks; the open and the closed; those she rejected and those she dug. But these were covert. Upfront we were all even-stevens – or else. Through her influence the PNP list was thrown open to all. If you wanted to be on it – in you went. It grew to include hundreds. As a result its identity definitely changed. For better and for worse. Jenny was happier, I was less so. But I let it roll. Probably I couldn't have stopped it. Still, in practice, the nourishers on the list were the ones most called on. Naturally. People know about satisfaction. But perhaps were weren't supposed to give it, for doesn't it create a hierarchy of giver and receiver? – bad news for the Great Equalizers.

So David Eddy was in demand whether in small company or among the host. David gave of himself and it was this that drew others to him. You would come away from having had time with him feeling yourself uplifted. There was something about him that made others feel good. He made you feel that you mattered, that your life was important, vital, that your self-realization was of the utmost significance.

Jane Eddy, his wife, never entered PNP completely. She attended many meetings and did much for those visiting her home. She was generous, she put people up – for days. But the emotional commitment was never entirely there. A discretionary way of seeing the world kept her both unattached and defiant. Setting out from her sympathetic standpoint she stopped on her way to weigh up the case and the demand on her inviolability. Fortunately this provided us with an objectivity we otherwise might have destroyed.

David and Jane were coupled. It was a snare for both. Under the surface of their tense serenity they fought like Kilkenny cats. Like many couples, together they colluded in a kind of horror plot. Each became aware that the other was the one kind of person that aggravated. Each would accuse the other, silently, in the heart, of causing pain. Each was unable to let go. It was much the same with Pam and me for a while. Nothing could be done but watch these two persons

I loved tear each other to pieces without a murmur – on either side. Finally they parted, and moved to become the persons they really were.

Others who were seen as giving much needed strength and confirmation were Mike Williamson and Bill Young, and Frank McAllan. There were those who came who had lost all sense of self as a source for these things. When it was rediscovered in the company of someone much respected it provided a new lease of life. Something, or someone, was needed to help numbers of people through the hoop of insignificance and sense of failure in our goal-oriented society, to restore to them their sense of worth and value as human beings with vital functions and potentialities. Our society extends little sympathy to losers in games that are rigid and settled well in advance.

The Neilsons, David and Cathy, gave something different : love and space. They provided a home for the spiritually homeless in the way they opened their lives to all who came.

At home Pam and I – and Shem – were full of callers. This was where it all began. And still, this was where one went to discover about the lines of PNP communication. It was the hub. Besides, Pam had a great deal to offer in the way she related to others. It was unusually natural. She could afford to be straight and honest and unsentimental because she had an essential love unadulterated by phoney ideals. She could be a tough customer sometimes, but this was part of her essential humanity. She did not have to flout this, since she had it at her disposal.

For the first half of 1970 the Friday meetings were held each week at our home. It became a regular feature of the underground scene and people would drop in throughout the evening who were engaged on various fringe activities, as well as those there solely as part of PNP. It was about this time that P Squared made its bow.

This sensational attempt to gather together all progressive activity : art, theatre, play, media, politics, communes, drug experiments, humanistic psychology, PNP, yoga, meditation, and so on, was the bouncing brainchild of one, Harry Pincus, a huge dangling, dawdling, drawling American who burnt himself up very slowly for a while drumming up together various freedom fighters for a new life, and experimenters in new fields. The name came from a suggestion from someone that nobody liked, but which, nevertheless contained the essence. It consisted of two words – I forget which ones – both beginning with P. So, $P \times P = P^2$.

Harry organized a number of marathon meetings at which everything was discussed but nothing was settled. One problem was that Harry's visions outshone human frailty. For instance, he said, P Squared needed a huge house in Hampstead, say, large enough for all these things to go on under one roof. Someone would ask the obvious question : Where was the money coming from? For Harry this was a detail. The money would come. One had a feeling he believed people would fight to donate it. Harry was way ahead; already allocating rooms.

Despite the high-stepping extravagance of these meetings, people kept attending. Including me. I found it very difficult to say No to Harry. His enthusiasm and faith were so towering, his aims so unimpeachable, that I had the sense that to refuse him was to be a patron of the Devil. Others who kept coming were David Cooper, Bill Grossman, Peter Paine, Keith Musgrove. Sometimes Harry, for lack of space, would decide to call a P Squared meeting at my flat on a Friday night to coincide with the regular PNP meeting. This would be bewildering. P Squared people would get up and make speeches thereby completely fazing the PNP people, for in PNP no one gave speeches – except me, once or twice, right at the start. Once over a hundred people descended on our flat, which is quite small. It was chaotic. Musgrove got up and said why he was there, a declaration that completely mystified the PNP people, who couldn't have cared less. When some of them told him so Keith looked amazed and asked where he was. And so on. Yet beneath the crazy chaos there was a marvellous energy, a sense of new horizons way beyond the boundaries of our immolating society.

Finally P Squared disintegrated. Harry moved on to a new

venture – Sanctuary for American Refugees from Conscription in Britain, and set his machinery rolling on his usual colossal scale. Every prospective MP (the election was impending) was to be questioned about his stand on the issue. Television would plot the answers on a huge board. A team of experts would discuss with Harry the import of all this. It could become the central issue of the election. Once, in a vegetarian restaurant, he sat plotting an assault on the English public about this question, outlining his strategy to David Cooper, Clancy Sigal, a few others and myself. He used to make me drymouthed with his projects. They seemed so crazy, impossible, doomed. After that small meeting the tiny group went out and started to canvass passers-by for signatures in favour of opening Britain as a draft-busters' sanctuary. I couldn't join them. I need a target that is at least feasible, otherwise I go numb. To Harry, finally, I was chicken, a bound man limited to the *possible*. He wrote me off.

But P Squared had its fruition. First, from it, Centre 48 was formed. Under one roof operated Reichian Therapy (Musgrove), Yoga (Paine), Encounter (Grossman), and sundry other activities too. This paved the way for the organized growth centres that came later. The spade work was well done.

Nor were Harry's extravagant dreams entirely unrealized. After Centre 48 atomized, Bill Grossman set up the Kaleidoscope Growth Centre in a house obtained from the Situationists Housing Association.[2] Here, under one roof, you can find many of the things that were to be included in Harry's dream house. Early in 1972 I joined forces with Bill Grossman. I am glad and happy to be part of it.

And it was at Kaleidoscope, this late deposit of Harry's dream world, at a party to launch its 1972 summer programme, that I heard of Harry's end: suicide; he had hung himself in Canada.[3]

How do we know that without Harry's dreams Kaleidoscope would exist today?

The PNP meetings grew in importance to network mem-

[2] See below.
[3] I was misinformed. Harry died in New York.

bers. But the essence of PNP was still contained in the list, the telephone numbers, the personal visits, the intimate exchange. We all had our regulars, who became part of our lives, mixing with our worlds, our friends outside PNP. A few were regulars to several of us, a handful to most of us; these used PNP for what it potentially was – a scattered commune.

'Judy' flew in from Canada, wanting therapy with the only man she believed could save her – R. D. Laing. But Ronnie Laing was the idol of many and so could not offer her time outside a consultation. He recommended someone to her. But Judy soon moved on. She did the rounds, tried one therapist after another. By the time she reached PNP, two weeks after arrival, she already had eleven therapists under her belt. None of these had offered her the food she needed. None had perceived her predicament. She did not want to be told what to do, or 'where she was at', she wanted to be *seen*, and to be understood. Why did therapists want to control her and run her life? She wanted only to have her situation acknowledged, her agony perceived, her despair appreciated and accepted. Nothing could make her happy since she did not seek happiness but the recognition of the extent of her personal disaster. All the therapists she had seen she saw as attempting to take her out of her agony to where they were, whereas the only way she could open to you was through your entering into her macabre world of total shipwreck in which she was irredeemable and damned.

Judy talked and talked without ceasing, annihilating any interruption. If I spoke, or began to, she would cut me off at once with a 'You don't understand', a phrase she handled like an axe. Any sound or move from Shem, and he was fixed with a look of hate. He fled to bed. Pam, whom she assassinated by total disregard, left for the kitchen, and stayed there. Me, I was her listener, and she gripped tentacularly.

This, as I saw it, was what was happening. Judy was locked in her own nightmare. When she shook free of it she talked all the time of it and so stayed in it. She had become her own nightmare; or at least identified wholly with it. Therefore any

162

attempt to dissolve it, or remove it, she experienced as a threat to her very existence. Therapists had talked to her from a land in which her nightmare did not exist, but such a land as this did not exist for *her*. To reach her, to confirm her, you had to confirm her nightmare, otherwise you would be rejected as a destroyer.

Gradually the nightmare itself began to take shape. Her fear was that she was *flawed*, flawed that is in her essence, in the very seed that conceived her. Hence she was beyond salvation. Nothing could be done. She was foredoomed to a flawed life, a defective existence. She could never be a real person because it was fated from the start that she would be incomplete, less than others, *no matter what*. For years she had been obsessed by this idea, was completely trapped by it. It was perfect. It was flaw*less*. It was the derivative of total despair, and its antecedent too. So long as she stayed in her head she was done for, like Kierkegaard, for indeed despair can be 'the sickness unto death' – if you are locked in your head. Judy had built herself a maze with no way out to play in and could not stop, though the maze did not exist. When I was in Australia I read about a murder in which a man's legs were pulled up behind his back and tied to his neck so that as he grew tired and his legs dropped he throttled. Judy had done this to herself, and then forgotten it was just a game and there was no rope. None of us is free of these sinister pastimes but Judy's was more sovereign than most.

After two hours, two and a half, Judy was still talking, I was still listening, but with my mercy strained.

I sat cross-legged on the floor and asked her to come, sit opposite me. 'Why?' she asked, and 'What's the game?' but did. I said to put our hands on the other's shoulders, close eyes and touch foreheads. Protesting, she did this too. 'Now what?' she said. Now nothing.

After about two minutes she broke away, looked at me, opened her mouth, but no sound came. A minute went by, whole and soundless. Then she tried again: 'but . . . yes but . . . what the. . . ?' – a coughing engine. Then it roared into life and she was off, the full flow, lashing me : What was

I trying to do? I was attempting to trick her, to move her away from her truth, her reality, her pain. Since *that* was real, what she had just experienced – good feelings – was not. On she went, as before. Later I asked her to do it again: the sitting and the holding. She agreed quite quickly. It was a long time, this time, before she broke – about ten minutes. It seemed like a miracle. As we sat touching I felt her relax, the tension flowing into me and out. I felt the beginnings of a letting-go of her defences and her desperations. Afterwards she sat where she was, looking at me silently. This went on. She seemed very peaceful. No words came for a while. Then the stuttering started. Then finally, 'That felt good, really good. I haven't felt so good in years. I don't understand. I feel great.'

But soon the rejections came again. It had to be unreal, since the nightmare wasn't. Burying her head in the sand, she complained it was dark. But then the light blinds, as we all know.

It was no miracle, but perhaps a flash that gave hope. And the flash had come through contact, including the physical, with another human being. Could a flawed human being feel, even momentarily, full and unflawed? That was a question Judy had to answer now. It was a chink in the closure of despair.

She came back often. She went to see Mike and Bill a lot, also Frank. Others too. She began to let one or two people in. No longer watertight, she let herself flow and found she could float. People grew fond of her, to appreciate her intelligence and her strength. Then she vanished.

Months later I met her by chance. She was fat and looked happy. Relaxed as well. She was living in a commune, she said, with David Cooper and others, and things were going very well. She felt good. She brought up PNP: 'A few of you on the network really helped me, you know,' she said. 'Two or three of you really seemed to know what was happening inside me and that meant a lot to me. But those shrinks! They kept telling *me* where *I* was at, and they never knew, and couldn't leave go of their own ideas for long enough to

164

find out. At least the people on PNP didn't do that. They let me be where I was. Then when I felt some of you could come on my trip with me I reckoned it couldn't be all that bad. Yes, thanks to all.'

Tiffany was a woman of some renown in psychiatric circles. She had been in many hospitals, and had received treatment of all kinds. Labelled schizophrenic she had a history of ECT and a welter of drugs that stretched across years of her life. She had found no way of saving herself from this fate. Unable to join in with others on their terms, she had led a life of uncertainty and fear, relying on hospitals and specialists to provide her with the necessary fortifications against her pain and against the threats from others to burst through her barricades. The schizophrenic syndrome.

Unable to feel like others and beginning to find out about herself, thwarted by herself in her attempts to live, she was undergoing a relationship with others that she could not often handle. Bouts of desperation drove her over and over again to seek the help of psychiatrists. But they failed her. Tiffany needed herself, but no treatment devised by man scientifically could lead her there. Only people. Perhaps.

She came first to see us with her boyfriend Chas. She had to leave herself behind for she could not believe that if she did not she would be allowed to be. Time and again she came, always fluttering through our lives without ever reaching the point where she could turn to us and be.

Chas cared for her and loved her winsomeness and her electric disposition. She could spin a skein of electrifying beauty with her delicacy and her way of reaching out to whatever entered her universe, great and small. Nothing could be left out. Soon she would become herself, falling forward into it, leaving behind her pretences and her bowls of behaviour that had been foisted upon her by those who thought they knew how to be. For her.

A matchbox, a match, a petal, a piece of cork, a shaft of sunlight, crumbs on the carpet – all these were received by

her with wonder and delight. In her world of utter involvement she was a finely tuned instrument that *missed nothing.*

She would dance extravagantly, gracefully, beckoningly,
devouring your attention for her movements – mark the
hands! – and her grace. Out of a splinter and cotton wool
would come a rag doll; works of art would appear out of
nothing. She would draw on a milktop, write a poem on her
wrist, switching bewilderingly : poet, painter, dancer, nymph,
brat, flapper, woman of the world; and only the last was a
farce.

But taking in like Tiffany did from the world needs a constant outlet and Tiffany was desperate for an audience. She
drove for people like a polo player drives for goal – she excelled
at overstaying her welcome. Nobody could hold you to her
more adhesively. She could make you feel trapped but unable
to move because that would mean dragging around a burden
of guilt for failing her, in so much need.

Tiffany would come again and again and stay until she
exhausted us so that we would get her to move on to somewhere else on the network, so that eventually Tiffany's day
was spent moving from one port of call to the next. Tiffany
wanted to be as important to you, whilst you were with her,
as you were to yourself. That sounds like a manifesto of love,
but who can follow such a manifesto by rule or order? It has
to come spontaneously from the heart.

Yet Tiffany needed it, to fill her hole inside her. Needing it,
she felt wild and rejected if she did not get it. This antagon-
ized other people, and made them offer less. They began to
be out, to say No to her. And Tiffany grew furious.

PNP was there for those who wanted what it was. It could
not alter to be what others wanted since it was what it was –
those in it. Soon Tiffany began to see this : that she could get
much from PNP but not all she felt she needed. For example,
accommodation. Once Tiffany separated from Chas she
seemed to be many times lost for a roof over her head. She
wanted to use PNP nights as well as days, and often succeeded.
So she came to rely on it. This led to the usual decreasing
circles of availability. More expectation, less offered, the less

offered the more indignant, and the more of that the less again was offered. And Tiffany would get stuck. But she could be loved, remember.

We often heard from her mother, who could not have her, for she was living where she worked. I think it was even more complicated than that. She would ask us what we were doing with Tiffany. Sometimes she would ring and say Tiffany was there and where could she send her? She did not push but would have been glad had we been able to take Tiffany off her hands.

She would freak out now and again, Tiffany, and go into hospital. Usually she would ring us from there and tell us bitterly how awful it was, and what should she do? She was not above using our dislike of institutions as a mild form of blackmail. She would ring me and say, 'Where can I stay tonight?' and I would say that I didn't know. 'Where on PNP can I go?' 'You have a list, Tiffy. It's up to you to find somewhere. I can't speak for anyone else on the network.' She would say, 'They're all out, or busy, or can't for some reason.' Silence. 'So where can I go, Mike?' 'I don't know.' 'Then I'll have to go back into hospital.' By this time I would say, 'That's up to you, Tiffy. It's your choice.' Then would come the twist. 'I thought PNP was there to prevent people from going into bins?' This would be said a bit viciously. But after a while it became a rubber knife that bounced off me. Finally Tiffany would apologize. If she didn't she would ring back quickly and do so. She couldn't afford to burn her boats, for she hadn't yet left home.

But then we found her a new one. She moved into the new PNP house, the second. This was after a number of events for her, including giving birth to a baby.

She had been there some months when I called to see her. She was very happy. She told me she knew how difficult she could be but the people in that house really accepted her. She knew she got on their nerves sometimes, but she had her own room and could retire there. We looked back on PNP. What had it done for her? She said, 'I saw two policemen beating up a Polish guy and I said to them, "Stop it. You're behaving

167

like a pair of skinheads." Then I was at BIT last week and there was a fire. Instead of panicking I got some water and put it out.'

?

She explained to me, her dumb friend: 'PNP taught me that there are not two sets of people in this world, the helpers and the helped, but one, all of us. We are all helpers and helped all the time.'

Out of the kitchen, into her room. On the wall, a painting. A yellow square. She saw me looking at it. 'Do you like it?' she said, laughing delightedly. "It's got nothing on it! It's just a yellow square!'

The king has no clothes on, cried the little girl. Make that girl a princess.

For a while, after splitting from Tiffany, Chas would visit Pam, whom he loved, for she felt for him and he saw. Here is a letter he wrote her:

'To my good friend and Spiritual adviser Pamela.
Hallo Pam.

I received your letter this morning and I will arrive there Tuesday evening to see you and Jenny James. I Bless you and all of yours for your kindness to me. I love you spiritually. I have got about £50 now so if you wish maybe we could all go sometime to a film or a theatre or just for an evening out. I would like to bring you a gift. I am still studying Indian tribal religion and customs as I feel a very deep spiritual kinship with North American Indians. I would like to fast until I die, or go into my next life, I feel I am a burden on people here, and also I am dishonoured and it is more noble to die than to live degraded. All my love to you and yours.'

The neatest cures are those that take place naturally. Next in line for thoroughness and reality are those that take place outside institutions. But not always do people find the way. Sometimes the situation is such that no known method will lead to the reversion of a disoriented life to its centre. Moreover it will be apparent to anyone that nature sometimes fails to right itself. This view in individualistic. From a total view everything always fits. Here is only the humanistic perspective : individual man as the ultimate value.

Never is it fruitful to leave out the first principle of active existence : nothing can be done without first finding the way.[4]

Near the very beginning of PNP's existence, when Celia, an art therapist, was part of the network, a young man George was sent to see us. He was an inmate of the hospital in which Celia worked. Celia liked him, suspected his potential, and was upset by the way he was being wasted, and wasting away, in the hospital which he lacked the sense of meaning in his life to leave. George was the illegitimate son of a Nigerian father and an English mother. He had been reared by Dr Barnardo's, and schooled there too. At fifteen he had wanted to go into the world, so he left. But he found himself at the mercy of rules and modes and attitudes he had not assimilated. Bewildered, he soon fell foul. Result : hospitalization; and an identity granted in this huge whirling social universe – mental patient.

George had never had to fend for himself before, not for basic needs like food and shelter and clothing. But once these were taken care of he had a way of making the best of a situation. So he thrived in hospital. He would go into the world, sure of his base, and transact there, and back in the ward. In this situation he was an operator. Without the basics *provided*, though, he was a man without the earth beneath his feet, plunging in a tail spin – as we found out.

That first afternoon he came over, quiet and docile, he watched us, felt us, drank tea, smoked, listened to pop records, played with Shem, all in a near dream. We all walked out for a while. George was tall, dark and remarkably handsome. People looked at him. But I don't think George noticed or looked back. His eyes were opaque; not seeing but fearing. The world was full of hate and would hurt him; nothing good would come out of it. Love, I sensed, was just a pain in his belly, a longing for his natural rights, not yet met. No mother

[4] 'There was a crooked man, who walked a crooked mile.'

169

had given him that sense of relaxation in which the world can be explored *at rest*.

We told George about PNP. Those were early days so we may have overdrawn it, made it seem a haven from his death in life. Or perhaps another kind of institution, fantastic, warm, and without rules.

Out of this meeting came drastic action. George rang the very next day to say he had left hospital and what should he do now? Our reaction, then, was to accept responsibility, in part at least, for the situation George had placed himself in. He came over and stayed a while and we armed him with a PNP list and suggested he use it as often as he wished. We fixed him up with somewhere to sleep the night. But the list had little meaning for George : names, addresses, phone numbers – words. He knew us. We had accepted him, let him in, and so he came to us again and again, always reluctant to leave. Pam was good to him, but I less so. I enjoyed people coming, but I also liked them to go. I was offering a service, some of myself and some time, but not a shared existence. I needed to feel I could move freely around my home doing as I wished. I did not like pulling in my horns. Besides, our flat was small. It did not allow for many different activities going on at once. And George always wanted on music.

We would draw him a map to another PNP address, go over it carefully, ring up and give news of his impending arrival, and send him off. But he rarely reached anywhere. PNP might as well have been on the moon for him, outside us.

Eventually he met others on the list at meetings and began to spread his sweeping needs over many. His way was to arrive, settle in – like someone in a Pinter play – as if he *belonged* there. To budge him was to give him a sense of *outrage*. Whilst with you he would eat like a lion, drink torrents of tea and coffee, smoke any cigarettes around, and use your home like a part of himself. PNP, or its people, were being put to the test.

It failed, if George's happiness and contentment were the keynotes, the measures of success. Soon he was back in hospital, in Bexley. David Eddy and Pam went to see him. Then Jenny did. Jenny then was squatting in Lee. She had converted a condemned house into a home for Becky her daughter and herself, and had already taken into it a few PNP homeless. George joined them.

George adored Jenny, and Jenny offered him a lot of love. He would follow her around, do chores, basking in her acceptance and the sureness of her step. He would become in part a child. When Jenny was away, as she sometimes was, the position was less pretty, for then George fell into a torpor, would do nothing, and would eat any food around as of right. This aggravated the others, since he contributed nothing. Somehow he always had some money, but this he spent on clothes and smokes and pot. He would ignore all protests, but lie around awaiting Jenny's arrival, whereupon his world at Lee would whirl again.

Then when I left for Birmingham Jenny moved in with Pam. George was left in Lee to fend for himself. He would make frequent visits over to Hampstead to see Pam and Jenny : twin mothers, sisters, loved ones. He was no trouble. He would play with Becky and Shem, listen to Pop and be happy. But at Lee the situation deteriorated by the day.

A little before Christmas 1969 all those bar George in the Lee house crowded into a telephone booth, rang Pam and me and said, in turn, if we didn't come and take George away they were going to kill him. I believed them. Apparently he was eating everything, offering nothing, and refusing to change his ways, or even discuss it. They said they would ring back in an hour to see what we had arranged. Three times they rang, without their anger abating. The third time Jenny was with us, visiting. She agreed to go get him, and this she did, with Nic Saunders (author of *Alternative London*). For a while George stayed at Nic's, then he moved back on to the PNP round again. When Jenny was not free, Pam was George's anchor, so he called often. He was dragging more than ever, almost a dead weight. He was invariably stoned, an incapable body. Finally David Eddy made George a grand offer. Apart from the flat he shared then with Jane, David had a small room in Belsize Square he used for privacy and writing. He

171

told George he could have that room rent free for a fortnight. In that time George would have to find his feet: get a job, or regular Social Security, and find a place to live.

George moved in greedily. As for his feet, he didn't know even where to begin looking for them. For two weeks he did nothing. We saw him because he used to come to Pam for provisions. We would urge him to get along to Social Security, explain carefully to him where to go and what to say, but we wouldn't take him there. We felt that would, in the long run, achieve less than nothing. He wanted to be taken over, but there were no takers.

So after two weeks nothing had happened. George sat tight, assuming his situation would last for ever. He was cruising. He had a place to lie and sleep, food to eat, and somehow he was mustering money to buy his drugs – no one knew how, but I had my theory. He was living proof of Newton's First Law of Motion: a body will continue to move with uniform motion in a straight line unless disturbed from that state by some force. If something happened to George, life changed; otherwise it didn't.

David asked for his flat back. George answered nothing. He was a daffodil, or a blank wall, or air, part of the air: a medium – words passed through him but did not stick or lodge. David, half helplessly, told George he could stay one more week but no more. But George was not to be caught up in this kind of ultimatum. As far as he was concerned nothing had happened. So life went on more or less as before: sleep, smoke, listen to music, make his purse, visit Pam and Jane Eddy and get some prog.

Meanwhile David's ancient shuffling German landlady was in a state of blank despair. George ignored her, or insulted her, when she made her requests for less noise, less mess, some consideration. She was giddy, lost. David was a perfect tenant, but who was this man, this insolent whelp, where had he come from, what was David doing knowing him, and what in God's name was he doing in *her* house? The one thing she knew was that she wanted him to go, vanish, disappear, anywhere and at once.

172

George was impervious to such moral pressures. He was owed a lot, and he was collecting his debts where he could. Otherwise, he moved if his body moved, and only then.

Five weeks of this marked the end of David's tether. On a Saturday afternoon he arrived at the little flat with Jane and told George he was leaving. George sat on the floor, his and David's possessions around him, listening to some records we had given him on an old record player of mine, demolishing a huge saucepan of hot potatoes. Eyeing them he said nothing. They asked him to pack. He did not move so they began packing for him. He watched them, munching his spuds, 'as if in wonder at these two human squirrels bustling busily about his flat' – as David put it later.

Then it was done and they stood waiting for George to move. He really was going they assured him. Finally George began to protest. He claimed rights as a sitting tenant, as a PNP member, as a sick person, as a man without resources. It was, as David said, 'a complete cuckoo-in-the-nest situation'.

David stood his ground, said enough was enough. George had to go. He sat in the back of the car, his saucepan on his knees, chewing his spuds. He began to relax. He was just going for a ride. He was with friends, with PNP, everything must be fine. David and Jane plugged him, where did he want to go? But George had no plans. What he wanted to know was, where were they driving him? As for himself, he didn't want to go anywhere. How to get out of that one? David and Jane made certain suggestions. He failed to react. They were in the West End by now. George said, 'O.K., drop me at the Arts Lab.'

In Drury Lane it was pouring and already dark. They stopped just in advance of the Lab and George grabbed his things and vanished into the darkness and rain, without a word. David and Jane sat in the car for a while, feeling much : relief, guilt, sadness, despair, much more. Then they drove on. As they passed the Arts Lab they saw it was closed. They kept driving. Then in agreement unspoken they turned back. Impossible to leave George alone in this weather if the Lab

173

was closed. They got out, searched the area for his tall sad form, but did not find him.

They came at once to see us, deeply moved. Jane sobbed, David fought off his tears. They felt terrible about what they had done. I was sure it was the right thing. Otherwise, where does responsibility end? And where, for George, did it begin? And when?

PNP was what it was, no more. It could not solve the world's problems. It could not help India's starving, smashed existences, cripples or, probably, schizophrenic disasters; nor, to his immediate satisfaction, could it entirely help George. But it was no less legitimate for that.

For a while we heard nothing. Then after months he arrived to see us with a friend. They were both in a mental hospital, and George seemed happy enough, as he always did in a way when being taken care of. His relationship with his friend seemed very real, with lots of warm feeling flowing in a style I had never experienced from him before, not even with Jenny and Pam. This was a human feeling as between men and equals. They stayed awhile, chatting and listening to music, then sweetly left. Another time Pam and I returned from a weekend away to find George in the flat with a friend. They had come to see us, found us out and climbed in. They had spent the weekend there waiting for us. It seemed right and fitting enough to him. He needed what we had and weren't using so he took. The logic of deprivation.

From then on events are less clear to me in George's PNP career. No one heard from him for a few months, and then he popped up again and told us he had a good job to go to Sussex. He persuaded Jack Lewis to put him up, and Jack nearly lost his flat and his mind. Within hours Jack was feeling a guest as George took over the music and the kitchen. Any comment was met with negligence or a flashing look. Then George began to wear Jack's clothes. Finally he added his ring and his watch. Jack, old PNP campaigner though he was, felt unable to intervene. George's smouldering fury frightened him. I knew what he meant. I had always felt it and had had nightmares about it in my time. But I felt responsible now,

174

God knows why, so I challenged George about the watch and ring. They were gifts, he told me, his eyes daring me to press it. I take some intimidating. In fact it's the best way of making me attack, whatever the odds. Reckless, I wonder how I'm so unscathed. So far. I told George I had heard otherwise. He insisted. I fed this back to Jack. Gifts? O.K., they are now, said generous Jack. And that was that. Eventually he got George out of the flat. He said it was only just in time. He would have gone mad. There was always a danger in PNP of acting the saint when you didn't feel it. Though it does little good in the long run we all sometimes fell into the trap.

George moved into PNP House for a while, where Jenny was. Then he left London, for Sussex and his job we supposed.

A long time passed without word. Then he walked in one day, his hair cropped, leaner than ever. His talk was more rolling, but nearly incoherent. Between snatches about the German army and parachutes and African wars we gathered he had been in the nick. He had knocked something off and been nabbed and put inside. He hadn't minded it a bit. It was better than the bin. I felt he was saying that at least he was treated as an adult, and not invalidated. He was finding it hard in the world. When he got tired he would do another job and get put in jar again.

He moved over to PNP House again. Jenny was away in Spain so he took over her room. Derek Russell, a Reichian therapist, who lived there, rang us. Did we think it was all right? He was being difficult but they thought they could cope with him. Then when Jenny came back she asked him to leave.

Who was left for him? Pam. He came regularly for a while and Pam would load him up with provisions and fags. Then one day he came when Pam had troubles of her own (with me). Pam the patient, the compassionate one, said, 'Sorry George. I can't talk to you. You can't come in. Goodbye.'
Et tu, Brute?

There were many new members of PNP by this time. He explored some of them, Peter and Val Dunmow, Peter Wells. Peter Wells put him up for a bit, but George no longer felt he belonged. He needed to be loved. Jenny and Pam had loved him, some of the others a little too. He was too tired to start again. He vanished. That was two years, two and a half years ago. No one has heard anything since.

Many Georges stalk this fragmented and alienated society of ours. They are the price we pay – or rather *they* pay – for our materialism, for our assembly lines, and also for our sense of space and self. When the tribe discoheres, and its members fight their own fight, many are lost in the wilderness. In our atomic anomic society that consists of sets and units we deal out untold unknown damage to infants and children, and provide nothing but institutions and patching ceremonies for these victims in later life. To return to an agglutinous commonality is no solution. Perhaps individual enlightenment, awareness and perpetual growth, leading, one hopes, eventually to a true and compassionate love, is the only way we can go.

Ned was soon coming regularly. He was coming to see if he could relate to others without playing the role of patient, I think. When he came he would try earnestly to get answers to all the questions in his mind, mostly about religion. He began to see that PNP was not that kind of association; that what we were was a group of people who wanted to relate evenly without roles or status.

For years he had been a patient of some kind or other. His parents had sent him to a variety of hospitals and psychiatrists, and also to more progressive attempts at cure. He had spent time at Kingsley Hall, that community experiment in the East End set up by Laing, Cooper, Redler and others. He had been in Villa 21, the project in Shenley Hospital run by David Cooper, and he had also spent time in Granville Road, another community stemming from Laing and his work. There had been various psychotherapists of different persuasions with whom he had worked at changing his relationship with himself and others.

At the time of the advent of PNP he had just finished a bout of this and was ready, I believe, to start making the attempt to stand on his own feet. PNP seemed a good place to begin. Everyone saw something of Ned. He went through various stages and seemed to change his style often. Sometimes I would feel he had reached a stage of inner security but then he would be uncertain and needy again. Patterns take some changing. Years of trying to relate to the world and others in new ways are often dogged with failure. It can take a long time before the breakthrough comes into a new style and a new certainty.

I felt Ned grew through PNP. Some of the members, like Neil Ormonde, befriended him closely, and helped his painful attempts to stand on his own feet by refusing to father him or look after his needs. He experimented a lot and bore the results. Gradually he came to see, as few do, that only he could truly answer his own questions.

When needing people, we feel shut out and rejected if they do not respond. When we begin to supply our own fulfilment we can allow others their own freedom too.

Eventually Ned moved into PNP House Two along with Tiffany and it was there that I went to see him. It had been some time since our last meeting and I felt very good about the changes that seemed to have taken place in him. He had developed, or found, a powerful perceptivity and a really sharp intelligence that was not so much clever as real. What he said appeared to come out of the depth of his rare experience, from a source far deeper than in most.

Whilst we talked before a huge log fire he would sometimes stand and stride around the room threading his long hair saying things like, 'No, that's not right' and, 'No, that's ridiculous' and, 'I can't tell you; I don't know how to put it'. Then he would return to his seat by the fire and continue, as if the saboteur inside him had again been temporarily vanquished. Here, more or less verbatim, is what he said; or extracts from it.

'For me PNP is the opposite of psychiatry, just the opposite. In psychiatry people aren't people. PNP cleans the air by turning everything around . . . turns it all around to where it always is. It is the alternative to the alternative. It is the real

M   177 reality. It's funny, what goes on and what has happened. It seems funny, everything has got turned round. Really it is psychiatry that is the alternative to what is.

'Does that mean love? Is absolute love demanded? Dedication, is that what PNP people need? No that's silly, if you take all that to mean what it is usually taken to mean. I mean absolutely anybody is welcome in this house. Ted Heath, Mr Crossman, anybody, but that doesn't mean someone can't ask them to go.

'I don't know what PNP has done for me. I can only say what's happened to me in the past two years since I first heard of PNP. I have come to see the possibility of being happy. That's it. I can feel its possibility even though I run away from it all the time. But I get close, I actually get close. It is definitely possible, I can feel it's possible. And because it's possible it's real . . . and because it's real it's possible. Now it's much more possible, much more real.

'You open the box and it's in the box, the box being the world. For once you are not afraid to open it, and there it is, all the possibilities, the possibility of being happy.

'I'm quite clear about all this in myself. But am I demanding of others that they should see it this way? You see, I'm not demanding of myself because it's what I believe. So I can't demand it of others. I can't do it.

'If I say I don't believe in psychiatrists it means I don't go to them for help and I don't suggest to anyone else that they go to them for help. I wouldn't stop them, I wouldn't suggest that they don't but I wouldn't suggest that they do either. I accept responsibility for this. If you don't believe in laws, if you are an anarchist, it means you don't steal, and you don't hit people over the head. If I do I am admitting the need for laws and for police and for prisons. . . .

'The idea that here are all the people in the world and they are all equal – that's a misused word – that idea seems ridiculous when you have to try and prove it in the face of alternatives. But it is what is and it is the alternatives that are ridiculous. . . . It's very difficult, for me it is.

'You know that's one thing I learnt from PNP – that you

can love someone and have complete commune with them whilst you are throwing them out. In a way their very act of getting me to go was an act of respect. They felt they could do it. At first this confused me, the way people whom I was sure, whom I felt sure liked me would ask me to leave because they had something they had to do, this or that. Then it didn't any more, and I saw.

'It all ties up with this reality I keep running away from. I've no right to talk about this reality because I run away from it and it is no good describing it, the only thing is to go back to it, back and back. If I got immersed in it I might have something to talk about. . . .

'When I was sixteen I walked out of school. My family, they are very liberal, very understanding – you would like them [laughs] – very much knew what the right thing to do was. They decided I wanted a change of scene so they moved up country. Then they looked round for a nice liberal hospital to send me to for cure. But I had seen a few doctors and that was enough, and I knew I didn't want to go into any ordinary hospital. But I was freaking out still and my parents wanted to do something, so they thought up Kingsley Hall, and I went there. There I did nothing – which is what I have done most of my life, only right now it doesn't seem so terrible. I didn't feel the Hall was doing me much good so I moved to Villa 21, Dr David Cooper's experiment in Shenley Hospital. That was no use because people were *put there* in the first place, they were not volunteers. And it was all part of the whole hospital system. What's the point of putting people into a box and then giving them *some* freedom? It's meaningless. If someone got violent or angry or freaked out they were *dealt with* by the nurses. There could be no commitment to what was going on. Everyone in the place saw themselves as being there because they were mad. It was cold, and it was an institution. So I ran away and went home.

'Back home I freaked everyone out. I can't remember the number of hospitals after that, most of the ones around York and Leeds: leaving them, going back, walking out, returning, transferring. At some point I joined Leeds CND and that I

179

can see was a very good thing. I made a lot of friends and became active. I liked it too. Then I moved out of my home and went to live at the house of the Secretary of the CND.

'Then I came down to London and went to see Dr Laing. At his suggestion I moved into his other community project in Finchley. Granville Road. In many ways that was a failure compared with how things are here in this PNP house. One or two people there were seen as being more responsible and capable. And there was a doctor, Dr Crawford, who was not supposed to be in control but who was on call, and he *was* called. And we all knew him as Dr Crawford. He was a doctor so I called him "Doctor". Something wrong there. Also I was seeing him privately for therapy. I liked him though. He was very helpful.

'Granville Road was better than any hospital, better than Kingsley Hall, better than Villa 21, better than the Outpatients clinic, better than home.

'But I moved out at the right moment.

'I chose to no longer go on seeing Dr Crawford. This was quite a feat. And I followed it up by getting myself somewhere to live.

'It was then, when I was living in Hammersmith, that I first heard of PNP. I had been there for a bit – no doctor, nothing, on my own. PNP was just right. People to meet but not to take me over. . . .

'It is never a question of just being given, I discovered that. People said they were going to help, and they did, but that didn't mean being suspended in sugar. It was a reality situation. There was a limit and that somehow was also the absence of a limit. Because there were limits the possibilities were limitless. I don't know, it's clear to me.

'Before that, you see, I had been out of contact completely. That's why I hadn't found this out before. You don't know anything for real when you are out of contact. But I had contact with these people from PNP. When you are out of touch you get the consequences of what you wrongfully hope for. If you hope for the wrong thing it is pain you get.

'All these paradoxes lie in the simplicity of the PNP idea.

180

'Most of the people in PNP said something like – schizo-phrenia, madness, paranoia, they were just labels. People were people. There was nobody they wouldn't talk with. The other side of the paradox was that they were people from whom not everything could be demanded. This was giving respect. When they asked me to leave I knew this wasn't rejection but accept-ance. They were accepting me as the sort of real person to whom that could be said. They were not treating me like a schizophrenic or a madman. If I said or did something they didn't like they said, "Ned, this or that isn't on".

'Some of the people living in this house knew nothing of PNP when they came. That's all right. You see it isn't really a PNP house, it's a people house. To call it PNP House is to label it. It's just a people house, a commune. You have to use the label PNP and then you have to throw it away. And that paradox itself lies in the PNP idea. That's why PNP is not an alternative. Everything else is an alternative.'

Res ipsa loquitor, as the lawyers say. The thing speaks for itself.

Twig

Outside London networks shot up and settled down. Leeds was the first city to form a network, out of the efforts of Ted Brown. Later the Whites, Mike and Jen, sold it further, linking it with other activities among those in the locality seeking new styles and horizons. Manchester struggled to find form. David Kaye made several attempts but failed. Then later PNP did become a reality there and grew to be part of the underground scene. In Birmingham two tries were abortive until Peter Waight soared on to the scene. Originally Peter came to interview me about PNP for the local newspaper, on which he worked. Roused by its possibilities he resolved to forge a network in that most ugly and unfriendly of cities. He wrote articles, advertised, probed around the University, and eventually succeeded in forming the largest network outside London. I was often in Birmingham during that period, and saw how Peter burned to get things going. It needs this from one, from several, to give a PNP a reality. Once it exists it can run to an extent under its own steam. But to give it birth – that needs colossal commitment :

Peter saw it rather differently : 'It doesn't take too much effort to be able to gather an initial – or even a large – group of enthusiastic people with telephones. The problems begin when you try and communicate to the community in which you live the information that such a network exists and, of course, why it exists.'

Moreover : 'The theory was that, after the initial effort, the network would virtually run itself, but in practice this was not really true. There is always a need for someone to be arranging the venue of the next meeting, the publication of the

182

next list of telephone numbers, and so on. One might think that these tasks could be shouldered effectively by a group as a whole, but in practice – in my experience at least – this is not the case.'

Some of the differences in experience relate to variation in scene. London has a strong underground. Once something like PNP breaks the surface word gets round to thousands in next to no time – and continues to do so, reverberating through personal contact all over the world. For London people, the experimenters amongst them, travel widely, and besides there is a global intercom connecting radicals, subcultures, the emergent futurists.

In no time we had visitors from Europe – Germans, Dutch, Belgians, Italians, mostly, but some from less expected lands. The Americans were naturally on to us at once – they have a nose for innovation, with their one eye ahead on the future (in eagerness or in fear). American accents were common on the phone, and mostly they would know at once the essence of the project. Explanations took seconds only; they grasped at once; they *knew*. Numerous reporters from various American cities came to interview me. In no time more Americans knew about it than English, I am convinced. I would meet people just over from the States, quite by chance, and like as not they knew of PNP. This became true in this country too, but it took longer and besides, since here *was* PNP, it was less surprising.

The only Frenchman we ever saw was Henri Gobard, a professor of Psychology and English in Paris. Henri knew Laing and Cooper and had translated them into French for his students – at that time there were no official versions. The students had been turned on and he had come to London to see that state of play in anti-psychiatry. He wandered around for two days looking for it. Laing was in Ceylon at the time and Cooper was living and sleeping in the back of a van parked somewhere in London. It was dark and raining so Henri said he didn't feel like tramping the London streets probing the interiors of parked vans with a torch looking for 'Coop'. Eventually he had been put on to us. He rang and arrived late one night armed, like a good Frenchman, with a couple of bottles of wine, and handfuls of anecdotes. Unable to stop talking, he opened my eyes. He found my Achilles heel, my murderousness. I might have killed him for his verbosity. Instead I said I didn't like him. Stunned for a moment he looked at me, his eyes pained. Then he laughed and said it was impossible. Since he had such good feelings for me, I *had* to like him. So, I soon realized I did. Besides, he gave me more space after that. It became hilarious. Pam and Henri against me, coaxing me, liking me into a trip of fun and spontaneity where things just happened and words flowed with joy and surprise.

Near the beginning, when PNP was just under way and Tarek and Alma were still with us and the movement was full of buoyancy and love, we were asked to do a film for Italian television by a team over here to take tape of a psychiatric conference in Edinburgh. When they got to London they met that lovely radical old campaigner Anni Soldi, so that inevitably they never reached Scotland but shot their footage instead at Laing and Co., and PNP. With us they set up a conference between five members of PNP – David Eddy, Mike Williamson, Tarek, Alma and myself – and two psychotherapists: an Italian progressive and an Argentinian, more orthodox, practising in New York. Through it we got some indication early on of the kinds of attitudes we could expect from professionals, both friendly and unfriendly. Objections and doubts seemed to fall under five main headings or questions: (1) What if a contact needed medical attention? (2) How would we cope with violence? (3) Was is really possible that such simple methods based on open relationship could heal and lead to growth? (4) Could not partial alleviation of neuroses and suffering dissuade contacts from seeking competent and informed help? (5) Could not 'amateur' interference actually retard development and cure?

Responding now: (1) There were three sympathetic doctors who had offered to see anyone we felt in need of medical or specialist attention, any time or day. (2) We were never called upon to deal with violence. If we had been we would probably have used Encounter methods to channel it safely. (3) Yes. We saw the evidence time and again. All neuroses arose once out of personal interactions with the environment and other people, out of situations seen as threatening, too painful, or beyond one's scope. Cure can lie in the reversal of these protective behaviour patterns, and the core discovery (as opposed to surface learning through the Behaviourists' methods) of new and more satisfying patterns, through fresh and less hazardous interaction. Other people might be both the way in and the way out. (4) What is 'competent' help? Where is it? How much of it is available? How much does it cost? Is the wholesale doling out of experimental drugs by doctors 'competent help'? Is the failure to see that drugs cause the organism to defend itself unnaturally, thereby destroying its balance, 'informed' intelligence? Or is it the beginning of the end of man's separateness from his inventions? Does it reflect man's deep wish to attain the simplicity of a machine, thereby dodging the responsibility of being human, that is, avoiding the pain of reaching the status of *homo sapiens,* judicious man? (5) Don't move; there may be a mad snake around. Could a fish swim if it could fly?

We began to get visits from further away too. From Canada and Australia, from Scandinavia, from Brazil. We heard tell of networks starting up in far-away places. We had drawn a line already sketched out in the new culture.

More networks struggled for life in other towns and cities in Great Britain : in Glasgow, Edinburgh, Worthing, Brighton, Nottingham, Bristol, Cardiff, Stoke, Hull. Some flourished, some withered. I believe Peter Waight underrated the efforts, his own efforts, to create a certain core, without which a PNP will wilt, or disperse, or die. The dynamic available for change, for innovation, in this fair land is limited. Britons take newness for threat. They like to feel that they will be the same tomorrow as today, like Big Ben. When they seek to change it means they do not want to be the same any longer. This happens seldom. Its tradition is based on 'character' – and that means fixed patterns and attitudes. This means that if you wish to innovate here you must be ready to be treated as

185

a joke or a threat or something for the State to take over. State-originated change is taken seriously since the State itself has a reputation for solidity and character. There may be grumbles but the State on the whole is to be trusted. Some people lump on to it the media, so any hopeful innovators must find a way at least of getting themselves presented in magazines and on television. These too are trusted and seen as part of the State.

But PNP with its simpleness and its lack of glamour was not readily accepted. Much work would need to be done to sell it to the general public. Which is a pity as it in no way belongs to an underground. No need to read Laing or wear long hair to fit into a PNP. You need time and space and a view of man that gives others their jurisprudence as far as possible, a gift for listening and a genuine concern for those suffering in the social jungle, perhaps silently in their hearts. No more. But party lines are out, and so are social sells of a generalized kind.

What makes it hard to build a PNP here is that people are not encouraged nor reared to think and feel for themselves. A stable society like ours depends on uniformity of thought on the big issues. It has its advantages, this. We have less internal strife and turmoil than most other States. But it does mean a stasis of social situations. Outside normality and usualness citizens turn to the State : to police, politician or psychiatrist.

In his play *Rhinoceros*,[1] Ionesco shows in excess the average citizen's reaction to what he does not understand or sees as threatening : first he tries to talk it into innocence; next he refers it to the State or the Administration; and if that fails he pretends it isn't there at all. PNP or rhinos sweeping the streets, in principle it is much the same.

If we are taught *how* to react, then how do we react to that which we were not taught how to react to?

Connecting us to our experience is our feeling; this is our unique responsive flow. But feelings have been largely outlawed. They are too inconvenient. They rock the boat. We

[1] See bibliography for details.

186

want order and peace – or so we are told. We pay the price of ourselves. Ionesco writes :

'. . . The Smiths and the Martins have forgotten how to talk because they have forgotten how to think; and they have forgotten how to think *because they have forgotten the meaning of emotion, because they are devoid of passions*; they have forgotten how to *be*, and therefore they can 'become' anyone, anything, for, since they *are* not in themselves, they are nothing but other people, they belong to an *impersonal* world, they are interchangeable.'[2]

With such people PNP would be a disaster. It would amount to a social pressgang, an insistence on conformity, in the face of symptoms *that express struggle against such devastating malpractice on the self*. So if PNP were to spread it would become necessary to vet members to avoid this kind of creeping manipulation. Or else we would end back where we started.

There is no PNP manifesto. There is space for numerous approaches. The Leeds group saw themselves like this :

PEOPLE NOT PSYCHIATRY

'Anybody that has had anything to do with the State Mental Health services will probably be aware of their gross inadequacies. Mental Hospitals suffer from all the drawbacks that limited finances bring. Staff are badly paid, with the result that people who might be interested in, say, mental nursing, look for better-paid jobs. One of the greatest faults in the system is the treatment available.

'Patients are fortunate if they see their psychiatrist for more than a few minutes each week. For the remaining period they are "treated" with an assortment of the pharmacists' wonderful products.

'There are pills to make them go to sleep at night, pills to wake them up in the morning.

[2] In 'The Tragedy of Language', in *Spectacles*, No. 2. Quoted in *Ionesco* by Richard Coe, p. 47.

'If they are depressed, there are pills to cheer them up. If they are too lively, there are pills to calm them down. Oh, how happy they should be! If by some mischance they were sane when they went in, they will be very lucky if they emerge still sane.

'If, then, someone gets worried, or anxious, he or she often lacks a friend close enough to turn to for possible help or re-assurance. If this worry persists, it shows. This society shuns worried people. Worried, lonely, people go mad. And so into the pill factory with the other nutcases.

'PNP is an attempt to stop this process at its source. We are a bunch of assorted people, interested in people. Most of us have been through some unpleasant mental states at some time or other.

'If you're hung up, frightened, lonely, or just interested, we could probably do each other a bit of good. People Need People!'

This was the Birmingham group's handout:

PNP

'Everyone has problems, fears, doubts: city life especially can be hostile and impersonal. Sometimes it gets too much to cope with alone, but there seems no one around to turn to, so often we resort to psychiatrists, drugs etc., when it is not really these we need. We're afraid to go to other people because we think they will turn us away.

'PNP is a group of people who feel that people matter. They are available for those who are finding things too much, but need people rather than psychiatry, a group of people who will try not to erect barriers, who will not push people into roles they don't fit. If you want to talk to someone (or if you want to help) give one of us a ring.'

Where many joined in one place networks were formed. Others wrote from isolated spots or from towns where numbers were not enough to form a full network. All letters were replied to. At times correspondences were set up. Answers

188

always included details of others who had responded in the same area. Sometimes these sets of links proved fruitful.

For instance, Jeff was lost in a Southern town and wrote :

'dear mike,

'i am writing this letter because i have a problem & need advice. Maybe i'm just imagining there's something wrong with me, but if so a little reassurance from someone would help immensely.

'i am a very orderly methodical person, i think, & am in complete control of everything, but i don't have any reality; it's very hard to describe. it's as if I were just watching life on a television screen. i can see it all happen but it doesn't have any reality for me, it makes no impact on me. when i'm with people i'm very unaware of what they're saying to me & i just mumble incoherent answers usually & so people find me a terrible drag, & consequently i have no personal lasting relationships, people get cheesed off with not making contact i reckon, they think i'm not interested in them. i would be if i could be, but it just doesn't happen, it's all just a dream to me. this all makes me lonely & i reckon that was the problem in the first place – living alone & never going out and i've just got more and more introverted or something, television hasn't helped, i don't suppose, – i lived with one for about a year.

'now it seems i'm permanently lonely with an eternal television & i'm very frightened & very sad. but as i said not so that i can't cope with life.

'this is a straight letter, no put-on, i really need help. could you give me any advice? would drugs help me find myself? should I go and *see* a psychiatrist? any help at all.

'please reply soon.'

Replying, we sent Jeff details of two others who had written from the same town. Both happened to be mental nurses. Both made it clear that they were not in favour of the treatment used by the State, but that they were forming their opposition deep in the heart of institutional lines. They were both sure that changes were coming, and were working to bring this about. We wrote to them, informing them Jeff might make contact.

Jeff's third letter came two months after his first. Here is part of it :

'I've been to see Kenneth twice and had long helpful chats and I've done an incredible amount of reading which has opened up a lot of good new scenes for me. . . . So I'm feeling alright now.

'I'm also working on a book of new poems, to be called, after some lines in your last letter, "Freshlooking Fields". I'll let you see it when it's finished, as it's thanks to PNP that I ever wrote it.

'Robin has replied at last and I'm going down to see him this weekend. Apparently he's very up on the poetry scene so we should have much in common. . . .

'I read your piece in *IT*. It was good. I hope everyone who ever gets into the state I did finds out about PNP before it's too late.

Thanks.'

The first letter had been in tiny writing, with small letters for capitals, including personal pronouns. This letter was typed and workmanlike, with proper Is. Before long he wrote again to say he and Robin had got on well and had met several times. Next thing was he had written to a University, and had been offered a place. On his way there he looked in to see Pam whilst I was in Birmingham. His next and last letter was from the University Union. It was mostly about a girl he had met who seemed to be in deep emotional trouble. He wanted PNP to help her. The letter flowed, the handwriting was a good size, and from it Jeff sounded a different man. There was time and room in him now to concern himself with others.

Amazingly simple. A few warm human contacts and a lost man, sick of himself, comes to life and moves into the world. Before long he is moving to do as much for others. Such may be the basic dynamic nature of a PNP.

190

Cloud

At the meeting I returned to that first time from Birmingham, after which my crisis in the family began, was Robin Farquharson. He stood out, dressed in a dark suit, a tie and a white shirt, from the casually draped people around him. He stood out because of his size too : he was a large man; tall, broad, with a magnificent head. His eyes and face are usually afire, yet that night they were not; they were soft and tranquil, almost demure. He must have been in a strange part of his being, or in disguise.

Robin had written to me soon after the start of PNP from a mental hospital in Pretoria, South Africa. Typically he had a copy of *IT* to hand there less than two weeks after it reached the London streets. He drew such happenings to him. Power surrounded him. Once it had been academic, this power. His scholastic achievements were exceptional. Many degrees, fellowships, awards, scholarships. Starred honours.

Then in 1966 he had dropped out, into the lower reaches of society for a while. A book tells something of his experiences.[1]

I sensed his dilemma was that he failed to see how he could realize his own full being in this world. Everything was against him, including himself. His power could find insufficient purchase in society to satisfy itself. Therefore he was forced to abandon most of it, leading to a stormy centre which took him from time to time into mental hospital. You might say he was invulnerable to social conditioning.

In his letter Robin referred to a Situationists Housing Association of which he was Secretary, whose aim was 'to get a house like Kingsley Hall except that it will have also people living in it who are not currently agonizing and who

[1] *Drop Out*, by Robin Farquharson.

191

can act as helpers, though there should be no rigid frontier. I would obviously be on both sides of whatever frontier there was'. He described himself next as being 'subject to manic upsets about two or three times a year' and explained that this usually led him into mental hospital. How long he spent there 'depends on how well-trained the bin is'. Finally he wrote, 'What you are doing needs urgently to be done and fits closely with what I have both needed and tried to provide.'

We talked of sanctuaries when we met that evening. Robin deeply wanted such a place and had committed himself wholly to finding it. He saw such an environment as providing him with the support he would need when he was freaking out, so that he could go through it, which hospitals did not allow, but blocked. Beyond his mania he might find himself, waiting. Society, normal society, refused to allow him to experiment like this, but a group of people committed to finding out whatever there was to discover would surely allow him full scope to explore his own areas of mystery and chance. He thought he would combine his renewed efforts to set up such a house with PNP's search for the same thing.

Houses for PNP, sanctuaries; we had hoped for months to find them. We had come up again and again against out limitations on time and space. We were human beings with individual lives who had only so much of these available to devote to others whose needs were often very great. This meant having to refuse, to stop something happening. For instance most nights visitors had to leave by twelve. Often this would happen when they were desperately trying to find their own being in a place where it could be held and loved. But at midnight or so they would have to collect themselves together enough to get home. And home might be a lonely pad without friends or hope. Time was needed by some of our contacts. A lot of time and freedom to move into new areas of themselves. We had tentatively tried to find a place, but to no avail. Our credentials were not sufficiently formal or impressive to persuade local councils to offer us somewhere for our needs. But we had never despaired of finding somewhere eventually. We felt it would happen sometime, since there was a

192

definite space in which it would fit. The concept was always being discussed. What would be its composition? Who would live there? Should we have infrastructure members there or, like Kingsley Hall, only those who were in chaos, and wanting to use the house for their own breakdowns and experimentations? If no one living there was made or felt responsible for the whole or for others in it, then it could find its own natural level. But then there were risks involved, together with the overwhelming question as to whether people in great need, or needing care, could really help and support one another, and move towards health and certainty. At Kingsley Hall there had been no interference from so-called helpers, little or no therapy from the so-called qualified and sane, but had Kingsley Hall really been a success? Robin promised to renew his efforts to persuade someone or somebody to offer PNP a house, of which he would then become a part.

For a while nothing happened. Robin disappeared from sight after negotiating alongside several PNP members with local councils without success.

Then I heard he had resuscitated the Situationists Housing Association along with Rhaune Laslett who was running the Community Settlement (now a Trust) in Notting Hill. Rhaune was on good terms with many councils and was likely to be able to find somewhere for Robin and others. But he did not contact PNP. Next I heard he had persuaded Leon Redler of the Philadelphia Association, and Anni Soldi, to join the Association's committee. Finally, more through them than Robin, I was invited to join the committee too.

I attended several meetings but did not relish them. There was a lot of talking, which I can indulge in like anybody, but really do not like. Rhaune would tell us about her work in some detail, which was invaluable – finding homes for people who would otherwise be in dire difficulty – like junkies and poor immigrants and solitary mothers. She swam in this work like a fish in water, smooth and easy. I liked Rhaune but felt a bit trapped by all the words. But patience paid off. Suddenly PNP had a house. Rhaune said there was a small mews house in West Kensington with a three-year life. It was in good con-

dition, and might suit, for a beginning, PNP. The committee
voted it to us there and then. It was not exactly what we had
hoped for. It was not suitable, not large enough, for the kind
of experimentation we so badly needed (we could have filled
six such sanctuaries with PNP people around this time). But
we could turn it into a kind of super-cell, a home for five or
six committed PNP members who between them could man
a phone and a front door around the clock.

Jenny James wanted to move in with Becky. Robin too, of
course. He had asked at once to be included the moment the
house was voted over. Yes, naturally. Without him there would
have been no house. Chris Cade and Graham Spowatt completed the initial contingent.

From the moment they moved in the world shuddered.
Robin, I heard, was going berserk. Nothing could stop him
from celebrating *continuously*. Like a lion let loose he went
wild. At once the balcony outside his window collapsed as he
lodged his iron bedstead on it to make more space in his room
for a party he was throwing for twenty or thirty people he
had picked up here and there – in parks, in tube trains, on the
streets. The house was full of strange people night and day.
Robin never slept, or hardly ever, and the stompings and bang-
ings and bellowings went on through the nights. Music
incessantly. His way of appeasing Jenny was to bring her tea
in bed at three in the morning then another cup at four and
perhaps a third at five. At six the partial peace would be
shattered by Robin's booming bass voice in the bath.

Then he would go out, carousing around the area in his
BIT vest celebrating the realization of his long-time fantasy –
a place for him to let go.

For a while Jenny stifled her anger, in part. There were
precious principles at stake. But then she began to ring us,
close to tears. Robin was impossible to live with. He had no
consideration for anyone else in the house at all. It was like
living with a tormented gorilla. She wrote to us saying, 'Who
will love the unlovable?'

Robin was working on Chris and Graham in strange ways.
They would come over to see us, at different times, in a daze,

194

baffled and amazed by their relationships with Robin. He seemed to be getting inside them, making them do things they felt were against their will. They were frightened, also fascinated, a bit stupefied by it all. They didn't know what was happening, but were excited by what it was. Robin was powerful medicine, and they were both feeling the power stirring and releasing in themselves. Robin had that faculty. He was a force.

I saw Robin only once during that first two weeks of the house's existence, and that was at the Inn on the Park, at a large party launching Quaesitor, the growth centre, at which many members of the Esalen Institute were present. Robin burst in dressed in his BIT vest and jeans, his feet bare over the lush carpets, and proceeded to invite about fifty people to the latest party to celebrate the opening of the first PNP house. His hair was tousled, his eyes afire, his energy bursting his boundaries. He began dancing, talking, declaiming, drinking, all at once. Then he vanished into the night.

Now that he had his house he thought everything could be. But PNP people, like any others, have limits, and these Robin transgressed at the house again and again. Some didn't mind sometimes; others permanently hated it. Jenny decided something had to be done. She called a conference, and rang Pam and me asking us to come.

Everyone was there, bar Robin. He was not excluded, just out. Jenny said, either Robin went or she did. Chris and Graham seemed fazed, they were indecisive, oscillating between agreeing with Jenny and awe and a kind of love for Robin. Both saw how hard he was to live with, a wild buffalo, but they saw too his magnificence, his power to light others up. With him their lives received a booster charge and they were loth to give that up. Also I was unhappy with the turn of events. PNP was for those whom society handled clumsily, rejected, or failed to understand. How could we in turn reject, eject? (It had happened already in Lee with Frank.) In principle I held that the house was a sanctuary for Robin, perhaps his last-ditch stand, and if others couldn't bear being with him then it was they who should go. But then I wasn't living there.

It was easy for me to have principles. And besides, surely this was where reality lay for Robin. Or is there no limit to what one person can legitimately impose on another while he is searching for his own natural balance, a search that has been agreed to in principle?

In the event, nothing was decided. The meeting was adjourned until the following evening when it was hoped Robin would have returned and be able to attend. Certainly no decision could be taken in his absence.

The next day Jenny rang to say that Robin had (at last) been picked up by the police and was back in mental hospital in Surrey. It appeared that he had been whirling around the streets in the early hours like a stoned dervish, had punched a policeman who had tried to interrupt his dance, and that was that. Back at the PNP house his things were moved into a corner and, by unanimous agreement amongst the tenants, his room let to someone else.

Within days Robin was on the phone to me from hospital. Somehow news of the events at the house had spirited in to him, and he was fiercely indignant. So he had been usurped? How could we do that to him? Was PNP welshing on its principles? Wasn't it through him that PNP had obtained the house anyway? I could only say that this decision was not mine. I was not a leader. I was not in a position to tell the residents of the house what to do. I had no jurisdiction at all, really. Perhaps my opinion weighed well, and perhaps I had not thrust it forward hard enough. But I felt in my heart that living elsewhere I was in no position to foist my feelings on to others and influence their living decisions. I felt sad about Robin, but there it was.

Robin forgave. He came frequently to the Friday PNP meetings at our flat. Sometimes he would sleep throughout, his huge form prostrate in the centre of the activity like a hibernating whale. Nothing would disturb him, not noise, music, people pushing and prodding him, stepping on him. At midnight I would wake him, and he would say thank you, and leave.

At other times he would arrive at the door out of the blue,

196

as like as not with someone or several people he had picked up somewhere on his travels, and they would eat whatever there was, and Robin would outline some enormous scheme he had. But although he had plenty of energy on these occasions, I always sensed a sadness in him, as if he was beginning to realize that *no one* could accept his full flow, not even PNP, not Pam and me. Perhaps not even himself.

He rang me up one night at about 4 a.m. to tell me he had just bought Centrepoint, that uninhabited architectural ghost of Tottenham Court Road, for many million pounds. Also he had been granted limitless power, and was prepared to fulfil for me three wishes. Tiredly I gave him three – end poverty, sweep the roads clear of cars, and turn back that year to the beginning. He rang back in an hour to say one of my wishes was proving hard to implement. Would I wait or would I prefer to substitute another? I answered him in a dream. Soon he rang again and wanted to discuss some detail, poverty in Haiti or something. I told him to fuck off and let me sleep, whereupon he exploded at my lack of faith.

It must be a year since I saw him. I heard he had joined the White Panthers and was using his power and magic in their cause. The last time we met he was very depressed. He had been brainwashed into believing that after all schizophrenia was organic and incurable, and so was manic-depression. He seemed to have resigned himself to a flawed life. I told him I thought he was copping out, letting go into hopelessness. He seemed to chirp up at this but also to resent it. If I was right he would have to start hoping and fighting again. Or so I fantasized. But this man, this giant, this mixture of David Cooper, Aubrey Beardsley and General de Gaulle, is, I believe, indomitable. Survive he will, I am sure, endure and come again. I find in me that faith in him.

Meanwhile PNP house was labouring, laden as it was with principles, PNP's and Jenny's. To Jenny, closed doors were *verboten*, a measure of the conflict and sickness of our society. We should all be open to all at all times – an unbelievably tall order, but Jenny was geared and game to try.

PNP house: surely that belonged to anyone in PNP? So

197

the wolves descended with the sheep and took as of right whatever was to be had. And the house lay under an avalanche.
Beneath this crush Jenny, smiling, tried to make her home,
for this too was important to her, and of course irreconcilable
with her doctrine of open doors, her principles of freedom –
to invade others at will (even if you did get thrown out). The
door stood open, swung to and fro all day as people came to
nourish themselves on whatever was offered. Also it was
assumed that here there was no curfew as elsewhere, so when
midnight came they sat on talking into the night, and then
slept where they were, on the floor, anywhere. Some would go
off for days and then return expecting to find their corner
available to them again, because they had left some belongings
there. Out of all this experience seemed to come a new Jenny,
more real, more truly honest. Principles were seen to be a
luxury in life, and experience the measure of reality. At least
that is how I felt her change. The house as home took at last
priority, and people respected this. This house was not an
open barn, nor a free-for-all, but a home for a few people,
and all others were guests and expected to conduct themselves
more or less accordingly. As guests they found far more scope
for personal freedom and expression than in most places, but
limits did exist and they were to be accepted and not transgressed.

The endeavour to change the tone of the house was pro-
moted by the advent of Jerry Rothenberg, a young American
who moved in with Jenny. For him people were not an un-
differentiated conglomerate to be socialistically approved, but
individuals to be liked or disliked, accepted or held at bay, to
be angry with or loved, or both. Gradually the house took on
a new tenor, of a highly ventilated home, a home open to
others on an uncommon scale, but yet a unit, and as such
able and liable to close when it wanted, to turn into itself and
be exclusive.

With this new stability things really began to happen at
the house in an ordered and useful way. It was one of the first
places in England to run Encounter groups, and this it did
free, twice weekly. Then Jack Lewis moved in for a while

198

and ran another 'on the house'. The groups run by Jerry and Jenny proved very popular, and many people involved in the Growth movement, as leaders even, would attend them and find them beneficial. Both Jerry and Jenny have natural healing qualities and are dynamos of energy. Their relationship flourished and they clearly gave a great deal to each other. Jenny in particular seemed to change a lot, and be closer to her immediate truth, leaving behind generalized principles of self and society. As Nietzsche wrote, one must have chaos in oneself to give birth to a dancing star. By chaos I see him as meaning no maxims, theories, *diktats,* and sundry guides to living, but flow, going with the moment, and no holding on to oughts and mights and wishful thinking. The general blocks us from the particular because it has already dealt with it.

Jerry Rothenberg is a man I admire very much. He has great sensitivity, a deep honesty, and an exceptional integrity. I have great trust in him. I also love him. At the time of writing he is undergoing Primal therapy, being perhaps the first person in England to have this intensive treatment designed to uncover all the *traumata* of our early lives, so that we can truly feel.[2]

In the meantime Jenny continues at the house, now almost three years since it began. Of the original group that started PNP, she is the only one still operating.

Sometimes I get the feeling that I created PNP for her, because for years she has been so naturally in it, of it, for it, perpetuating and energizing it. There is in her something I deeply respect. Perhaps one day I shall learn to love her too.[3]

Epilogue to Cloud: Dr Robin Farquharson died in hospital in April 1973. He had incurred severe burns from a fire in a derelict house in St Pancras, where he had been squatting with a group of labourers. He was 42. Three days before he died, after an interval of over a year, out of the blue, he dropped in to see me.

[2] The second is to be my friend and colleague at Kaleidoscope, Bill Grossman.

[3] Almost magically, this now seems to have come about.

Stream

At times I felt I had reached the end of my tether with PNP. Most days seemed to be filled with its activity, or else our separate lives had to be bent or fractured to let in some emergency event, or surprise caller. Pam and I were beginning to feel we had no lives of our own. Also, I was in a state of almost constant crisis with my marriage. This meant the energy I had available for others was far less than it had been to start with. But I carried on, feeling that PNP was vital to society, or at least to certain members of it. I wanted to believe too that PNP could not exist without me, I suppose.

After returning from a hectic holiday on the Continent, in which we had whirled through seven countries without once letting go the stored tension, we felt sure we could no longer continue. We had many things we needed to sort out with each other. There were crucial issues to be settled. PNP was in the way. Commitment to it held us fast to each other. Therefore we decided to pull out.

We called a meeting and announced our decision. From the silence in its wake came offers from several PNP members to take over the reins. We had been doing things that would require replacements. For instance, the Friday meetings had been held at our flat each week the whole year. Alternative arrangements were needed, for these meetings were valuable to many. Then there were the lists of addresses and phone numbers. These were still the main operational tool of PNP. They linked the stable centre of the movement with those in need and with those who were new. Also there were the calls. The telephone call was the initiating act of contact, usually. It was our number that had appeared in all news and information about the group. Most initial contacts therefore came to us. Our phone rang most of the day. We would like this to stop. We wanted a break from PNP altogether. We wanted to search the remnants of our relationship to see if it could be salvaged. We also wanted to rummage in ourselves. Helping others is a choice way of avoiding oneself. If only through others can oneself be found it is also true that only through oneself can others be found.

Peter and Val Dunmow stepped firmly into the breach, along with Neil Ormonde, Jack Lewis, David Eddy and of course Jerry and Jenny. A bunch of numbers was to replace our single number that had been previously appearing under *IT* Community Services. A letter was published giving details of the new set-up. The choice of numbers ensured that the burden was spread. The Dunmows in particular did their best to make our absence negligible. Their telephone was consistently the busiest in PNP for a long time after. It was very comforting for Pam and me to be so sure of them. Calls came to us for months after we dropped out for our number was widely known amongst people who floated in and out of the movement, using it whenever they felt a need or a want. Also, since word of PNP passed largely from mouth to ear, our number was being fished out of purses and pockets for months to come, and given to those in crisis. Most of these calls we passed over at once to Peter and Val. They also put out the list regularly and arranged a Friday night meeting somewhere each week. This varied, so that many had the opportunity to play host. Many other small local meetings took place on other nights here and there, so that for a while PNP flourished perhaps as never before, if in a somewhat different style.

The list grew and grew as it continued to include all those who wanted their names on it. Following the Jenny line, Peter did not vet these. Sufficient to want to in order to be part of the PNP list.

Soon after leaving PNP I wrote an article on it in quiet retrospect and this was published by *New Society*.[1] Included in it was a block of telephone numbers and these were used numerously. Unlike the original arrangement, when every new

[1] See bibliography.

contact was seen at first separately, most of these callers were asked to attend the next Friday meeting to find out what went on. No one seemed to have the time to present PNP individually.

Curious, and wishing too to help, I attended several of these meetings around this time. They were enormous, with up to and even more than a hundred attending. The new influx seemed very different from most members of the moment. Many of them were inquisitive, radical, or disgruntled professionals, and some did not take easily to the annihilating democracy of PNP. They saw themselves as competent helpers, and were looking for disturbed and distressed people on whom to practise their skills and express their human commitment. But by then PNP was not open, at least overtly, to this kind of stratification, and many of these new members left unsatisfied, and even piqued. But some stayed on to find a new way of relating to others in the soup that was not based on stands of professional understanding.

One of these was Peter Wells. Like Jenny, Peter was a PNP natural, though of a totally different ilk. He was in his early fifties, a dynamo of quiet energy with an ability to sustain interest in others over long periods, so that PNP callers found it consistently meaningful to return to see him again and again and grow through committed interaction. Peter seemed always to have space and time for PNP though holding down a full-time job as a psychiatric social worker and having a number of personal interests that also took time. His presence was invaluable to PNP at a time of uncertainty and change, and I felt his infinite reliability.

At first he was full of the ills of society, convinced that really little could be done about individual problems until the social scene was radically altered. Nothing much would change the multiplying individual sickness until such time as the face of society was transformed and it ceased to despoil its children and cloud their limpid lives.

We argued long on this. For me it is futile to act to change society, to pursue revolution without first changing individuals. If the content remains the same, the form can differ little.

202

It might have a new label, boom forth a new ideology, but a shuffling of the social pack is the best that can be hoped for. Commitment to a cause outside ourselves is absurd and sure to prove fruitless. And inconsequential too, for we do not possess that kind of power. Our ideals disappear into the smoke and fire, and ashes, of events. Turn belligerent, political, revolutionary energy towards transforming oneself, and then what? And think, the ground covered is consolidated, a real gain, not to be lost in a *putsch* or a corrupt administration. No one can rob me of my personal growth, *not even death.*

Gradually Peter seemed to change his perspective and become more individually oriented. This seemed to work towards himself too. I sensed him become firmer, more centred, more real. He began convening a Carl Rogers-style Encounter group for PNP members, and others, each week at the East London Encounter Centre. His quiet firm style led to much happening, much self-discovery. I respect Peter very much, and I have a deep affection for him too.

Tarek, Jerry, Peter, David, Jane – these were the people of PNP I came to love. Others too, like Tiffany and Ned, and Mike and John for a long time. But these five were special; they came from my selfish heart.

I can hear the question: wasn't PNP, then, an attempt to change society? In essence, no. It was a group of people connected together in the hope that this would help them to change themselves – eventually, their only requisitionable jurisdiction.

Those vast meetings after the publication of the *New Society* article were full of people looking for PNP. Only a handful of experienced members would be present: always the Dunmows and Kevin O'Sullivan, usually Peter Wells, Jack Lewis and David Eddy, sometimes Jane Eddy, Jerry or Jenny, or both; too few to present comprehensively the network's mechanics and intentions, so that lots of people looked lost, uncertain, bewildered, at a loss. PNP was in danger of leapfrogging over itself. There in part as a haven between the isolation of oneself and that other isolation – the false and impersonal network of relationships of society at large, it threatened to develop itself into a miniature society in which the choice again was to be alone or one of a throng far too large and intimidating to many. Faced with this crisis I hit upon the idea of the Trust Group.

I was convinced that it would be advantageous to all in this massive movement now if an addition to individual contact via the list and the large and fairly superficial meetings, there could be offered to all members and all new arrivals a chance to become part of a small group of people, say eight, who would meet regularly, on a weekly basis, there to thrash out personal problems and their own interactions in depth. I believed that if this were done, if it were persevered with by all its members *no matter what happened*, it would lead necessarily to new degrees of understanding of oneself and one's relations to others. It could become a new style of family, a family of peers that would not be imprisoning, but be based on the separate responsibility of its members to and for themselves. There would be no generational stratification, with all the false values and notions of predominance and right that brings. It would not be based on advice or instruction but on shared insights and direct and honest inter-relation. It might work beautifully. It might be a fiasco. It was worth trying.

I wanted to begin with a Pilot Group. I felt somewhat apprehensive about the possible productions of such groups and wanted to feel my way. I sensed and suspected the power of the group situation and I wanted to investigate thoroughly the potential capacity of a random group to deal with its own productions. My idea was that if the pilot group proved to be successful then its members could break up, each one convening a new group, and so on down the line until there were cohorts across the entire fabric of the network.

Peter Wells said at once he wanted to be part of the project. Kevin O'Sullivan said he would like to be included too. Kevin was a close friend of the Dunmows, staying with them off and on and doing exceptional work with a few PNP people whom he seemed to understand deeply and who in turn trusted him implicitly. I felt in him that natural thaumaturgic healing quality that seems to foster others through its mere presence.

Kevin knew well the committee members of the Student Housing Association and it was through this connection that we obtained the second PNP house. Kevin took Peter Wells and Jack Lewis along to meet the committee and speak of the work and aims of PNP. As a result the committee offered PNP one of their houses on payment of an initial deposit of £50. Peter wrote out a cheque and the house was ours.

It was a very different proposition from the first : squalid, ramshackle and dismal, and, to begin with, without electricity or gas, or even water. Nevertheless in the cold and dark of the new year (1971) Kevin moved in. Later others joined him, including Ned and Tiffany. . . .

The very first meeting of the Trust group took place in Kevin's room at the top of this house, with a paraffin stove for heat and a candle for light. Apart from Kevin, Peter and I, there were in this group David Martin, Julia Cayley, Shirley West and an American girl named Lily. It was an eerie evening as we boxed and sparred by candle light, throwing shadows of our forms on the wall, and of our real selves at one another. But it was exciting, knowing we would go on meeting, that there was no hurry, that we could afford to move gradually into the unknown of our relationships without fear of it disappearing before we had gained the courage to meet it.

Soon Kevin dropped out, since he didn't really wish to share his problems, or interact, with us. So we moved base to the cosy comfort of Peter's flat. It was perfect. Soon Sue, Peter's woman friend, joined the group, and so did Norma Rhaines, a doctor in sociology. So we were a firm nucleus of seven : Peter, David Martin, Sue, Julia, Shirley, Norma and myself. Some others came and went for a few weeks only.

Lily left quickly, after two or three times. But before she vanished she taught me quite a lesson. After that first group I found myself in a pub with her and heard myself ask her if she would sleep with me that night. She agreed almost silently and so off we went. I didn't go home. It so happened that this was the first time since I had been married, in nigh on seven years that is, that I had stayed out all night with another woman. Looking back, and considering the extent of my sexual gymnastics before I got married, this fact seems incredible. What a tribute to Pam, to her love and her sexuality! Once I made the break, with Lily, I was soon diversifying sexually again, but this first time I was amazed at what was happening, wondrously giddy, feeling myself carried along by a tide, that marvellous breathtaking sense of being hurled into one's future by forces so strong and dynamic that they break the arbitrary limits we impose on ourselves and the restrictive patterns of our lives.

I do not wish to imply that I was imprisoned by Pam. For years there was no urge on my part to go beyond her sexually. I chose my fidelity and was glad to do so. But that time had passed, yet I was still stuck.

During the night I talked to Lily incessantly about my marriage. Strangers are better than friends, often, for the intimate stuff of one's life, and if the stranger is lying in bed alongside you, the setting for confession is perfect. She was a good listener too – saying next to nothing yet being *there*, and alert.

Next morning I got up and prepared to leave. Where was I going? Lily wanted to know. 'Home, of course,' I said. 'I thought that was all finished for you, that you wanted to split?' she said. 'That's true,' I said. 'But still I have to go home.'

'But why?' said Lily.

I suddenly saw. I didn't *have* to go home, I *chose* to. I said, 'I have to go home because that's where I live. It's my base, where my son is, where my things are.' But I felt already the lie. What a farce; what hypocrisy! I had been complaining about my marriage, but *who to*?

Like almost everyone else in this age of hyocrisy and illusion, I said one thing and did another. The authentic act would undoubtedly have been not to return home, to have separated myself from it *then and there*. I could feel the terrifying possibility of this act within me. But I turned my back on it and left, and went home to Pam's wrath.

Well and good, if you like. But I had to stop pretending to myself that I wanted to do anything else. I had to see,

206

as Lily saw, that *my life and my self were one and the same.*
The rest was self-delusion.

That first (and last) Trust group became curiously important
to its members. It was rare for any of the regulars to miss a
meeting, and each of us came to see it as something precious
in the week. Julia would come back from holidaying in
Brighton just for it, returning after it. Norma would rearrange
her lecturing schedule to be there. Slowly the interaction became
intense and powerful emotional relationships developed between members. Anything that happened between those in the
group, in or out of it, was considered to be the property of
the whole group. It worked. Everyone really opened up.
Finally the group began to penetrate me behind my subtle
control and power, and my manipulation of its dynamic.
Slowly I too began to confess. I am aware that I capitulated
at last only the week before we were due to finally break up.

We broke up because four members were leaving London :
Julia and Shirley for Italy, Norma for the States, Sue for
Leeds. Before then, whenever we had remembered that we
were intended to be a pilot group, and to break up as soon
as we could and convene disparate groups, we had immediately forgotten it. We wanted very much to stay together.
We had distances to go with one another and we knew it. It
was a tough, tender, sensitive group in which members
exposed themselves to extraordinary degrees, more even than
in an Encounter group, perhaps because the methods were
gentler. They could afford to be for we met so many times.
And it paid off. Revelation moves like a waking snake.

The refusal of the pilot group to disband need not have
prevented Trust groups from spreading throughout PNP.
But who was to organize this? Those with the faith lacked the
energy or the time, or the confidence. In a way I would like
to have done it, but I knew it was out of the question. I would
feel tired at the very thought. Launching PNP had been
enough.

But the first Trust group was an unquestionable success.
I see the whole idea as having vast potential. It could revolu-
tionize society; solve, or help to solve, problems of isolation,

alienation, loneliness, family garrisons, schizogenia, as well as leading to a higher sense of self-responsibility and a far greater self-awareness. Well, that might be an ambitious expectation. But I see it as *working*, as curing some of the ills at least endemic to our kind of society. I have a fantasy that Trust groups, or something like them, will be a feature of the twenty-first century.

Sea

Someone in Ken Loach's film *Family Life* says, 'At least they know what they are doing.' 'They' are the psychiatrists, and the trouble is, they do not. But the real tragedy is that they do not know that they do not.

The history of psychiatry is the history of the error of experts, of ignorant practitioners and scholars.

In its time psychiatry has used as therapeutics: the feeding of iron filings to patients to give them strength against attacks; the replacement of human blood with calf's blood to produce calm; the inoculation of scabies to give the brain's corruption an outlet – through the putrescent scabs – the consumption of soap and tartar to purify the system; constant cold baths to cleanse of impurity; rotary machines to drive out melancholy.[1] As recently as the end of the last century castration was being used as a form of psychiatric cure. In this century, in the twenties, mental patients were being warned about the dire effects of masturbation.

Today, in our enlightened age, we have of course enlightened methods of cure, like leucotomy, electro-convulsive therapy, and drugs. Or so some believe.

Psychiatry has always sought the simplicity of scientific cure zealously, as if its reputation were at stake. Alongside this endeavour has gone the parallel pursuit of empirical cure. These attempts to codify man seem to be in our Western blood. Even Janov, the latest innovator, with his experiential creation, Primal therapy, now seeks a scientific explanation and a mechanistic method of applying his cure. Oddly enough, science disproves itself every time it makes a new discovery. It is one thing to say 'This much we know'; it is quite another

[1] See Michael Foucault, *Madness and Civilization*.

to say, 'This is all there is to know'. The progress of science is a refutation of its own dogmatism. But science seems to be no less dogmatic for that.

We feel this need to hold on to something, as fact, as truth, and will not let it go until we have something with which to replace it. In the East, some people know how to hold on to *nothing*. And they always seem so much wiser and more human for that.

That psychiatry today largely treats symptoms is a cliché. Symptoms, to an extent, can be measured. Causes, if they can be found, cannot. But man cannot be separated from his symptoms. He is one, a whole. Symptoms are signs, messages, expressions of the organism's activity. They may be healthy. A cough may be clearing congestion, bleeding cleansing a wound. They often have value to the person; reflecting his attempts to maintain balance. It may be that we neutralize symptoms at our peril. Signs will have their say one way or another, even through a cancer. The task is not to eliminate symptoms but to understand them, decode them.[2] Then if we are wise we will take action in the light of them. A simple example: my back aches; I ask it why; it replies – You are breaking me you are working so hard. I see that I am indeed overworking. I stop working; my backache goes. Another example: my lower back seizes up; I am paralysed, in a vice. I realize it is my own vice; I ask it why it is there; it says – Enough. You need a holiday. I struggle on for a week, bent double, getting regular massage; then I go on holiday; the vice opens; my body is free; it stays free.

There is always a logic at work. Sometimes it is intelligent, sometimes crass, or obsolete. I believe, I repeat, that all neuroses, and all psychoses even, are based on some kind of logic, usually primitive, infantile *and* obsolete, but very power-ful. Cure often lies in detecting that logic, seeing its sense and also its limitations, and going beyond it to a higher and deeper logic that will subsume and disperse the other. For instance, making schizophrenia very simple for the moment, we can say it is based on the logic that it is necessary to hide in order

[2] See Groddeck, *The Book of the It.*

to survive.[3] Once that may have been true, a child's experiential decision. Later though, superior logic may see that it is *no longer* necessary to hide, that the danger has passed, or can be now withstood. Finally, somewhere, I believe, there lies the ultimate logic, the pure natural system, the original energy, life.

Psychoanalysis, in its laborious way, attempts to reach these superior systems of logic, and through activating them and identifying them endeavours to disperse the neurotic systems. It fails because it almost entirely disergards the fact that the body and the emotions are also victims of the neurotic system or systems. This realization was at the root of Reich's work and led to his schism with Freud. It is also recognized by most of the new therapies, including Primal therapy – which *assumes* that emotions locked away in the body *are* the neurosis.

Not only the mind, but the body and the emotions too have to experience the freedom of open and flowing life, the release from the effects of imprisoning logic. *The ultimate logic is no longer logic but life.* This is where the mind and the body meet. The ultimate of both is energy. Here, logic disappears and there is only life. And life *is* energy, and energy life, and these know nothing of neuroses.

In workshops I am sure I have seen people reach this pure place, and whenever they do they laugh. From this ultimate perspective and freedom they look at their lives, at the years of games, of pretence and inhibition, at the long tragedy, the comi-tragedy, of error and waste, its absurdity and its pathos and its myopia, and they laugh; time and again they laugh. They laugh for themselves, for others, for you and for me, for the idiocy of our invented complexity that hides from us the simplicity and joy of just being alive.

This in a way is like the Zen experience, the sudden illumination, *satori*. But it does not last. That is the tragedy – or perhaps the entire explanation of our string of existences, if you believe in *karma* and reincarnation; for it is *samsara*, the

---

[3] Somewhere Beckett goes even further: 'Don't wait to be hunted to hide.'

day-to-day world and the selves we have fashioned for it, the selves that together *are* it, it is that which always comes back. I know as yet no way to make it endure, that experience, that illumination. Presumably, in Eastern terms, if it did endure you would have reached *nirvana*, and you would indeed be free of the round of birth and death, free of *samsara*, or maya – the whole world of experience apart from illumination; that is, illusion. The trouble with this explanation is that it offers the choice : be of the world and deluded, or out of this world and enlightened. I want to be in this world *and* enlightened, and for everybody else to be too.

But if this experience, in whole or in part, or if *the path to* this experience is the aim of true therapy, of discipleship, studentship, of work on oneself, if health is to be what we are all the time, and therapy the art of finding what we really are all the time, or letting it find us, if this natural experience is the goal, what is to be said for orthodox psychiatry ?

Leucotomy : this is a violent act trumpeting therapeutic failure : it is also a violation of man by man. Drugs are merely invaders keeping the restless natives down. They reflect (of course) the over-organized and repressive nature of our society. ECT : a brain-scrambling device that plays hit or miss, with human beings; a shot in the dark in the hope that it will hit a destructive system; if it does, what will take its place ? Analysis and psychotherapy are based too often, through the grid of a theory, on social adaptation and the renunciation of feelings. The way these methods are confined to the mind often, by my standards of health, prove disastrous. Analysts, therapists of the conventional kind, and those who have been treated by them extensively, are the most defensive and least free-flowing people I know. In Encounter groups they can be a menace as they soak up time with their convoluted talk.[4]

At least in the Human Potential movement there is hope.

[4] Bill Schutz writes on the subject of training Encounter group leaders: 'I concluded that psychiatrists were very difficult to train because they were very tight and constricted and did not have the desire or training to open themselves up as people and use all of themselves to help the patients.' *Here Comes Everybody*, p. 243.

To begin with man is treated as a whole person : a thinking, feeling being with a body, a field of dynamic energy all of which is affected by his every experience. Roles, pretences and defences are seen as standing, on the whole, in the way of man's growth towards his full potential. They may have uses, but these are secondary, as the moon is to the sun. Many of the techniques and methods used in workshops are highly effective in producing the kind of illumination that can lead individuals towards that goal that I have suggested as being the most real and meaningful for man. In other words, Gestalt, Bioenergetic, Encounter, Psychofantasy and Psychodrama methods, and some Yoga and Meditation methods too, I call 'good' because they foster the kind of growth I see as enriching man, and eventually society.

That they do this is due in part to the fact that they work with feelings, and when a human being is feeling he is flowing, he is on the move. On the other hand, too often when he is thinking he is static, or plodding his prison quadrangle, or being defensive, and thereby preventing flow. Moreover, deep feelings flowing in one person in a workshop set them flowing in others, and there is confluence, and communication of a very powerful kind. Persons flow together, act and react potently upon one another so that change takes place. People are entered by others, are nourished by others – and other people represent a huge sector of our environment from which we draw sustenance to *grow*. Workshops are phenomenology in action. Egos, false constructs, go, enabling individuals to move towards their essential nature, their ultimate. This kind of experience is at the root of faith healing and of miracles. It is based on the acceptance of the fact that there exists in each one of us, at our centre, a pure white light, a positive power, a life energy, that simply wants to be. To reach this, or let it reach us, is to attain the simple state of being what we essentially are. Here lies that life that remains Life even in death. For death is part of that Life, just as what we normally call life is part of that Life too.

As for PNP, it lies at the beginning and at the end of all this. PNP is for people, for the essence of interhuman activity.

It is for the sound of music they can make between them, 'a kind of song and not a wound' as John O'Shea wrote in his *IT* letter. By its very nature it is for the essence in man. This is a high-sounding phrase, but in its modest way PNP does attempt to get behind the defences and the manipulations that we have all manufactured as ways of dealing with the world we live in, and to reach what is common in man. And instead of considering people as things to be experimented upon, it see them as beings to experiment *with* – in new ways of being together. It tries always to see man as a whole creature, at least potentially and also in ultimate actuality. It believes man can be what he is through his own efforts and the contributions of others behaving naturally, so that any change will come through a movement of the whole person and out of actual experience, rather than through the thrust of reactive chemical agents or bursts of electricity through the brain. It rejects artificial attempts to cure, or rob, human beings of themselves and their history. It is also against the passivity of these modern methods. The experience of its members is that only those who are actually helping themselves can be helped by others. My experience in the Encounter movement substantiates this view. A neurosis is operated within the self, and can only be dismantled from a deeper level in the self, never from a more shallow level. Mechanistic cures achieve, in reality, nothing. At most they whitewash over cracked walls. The individual must be mobilized towards cure at a deep level, otherwise, like Canute, he is bidding back the tide. As Groddeck would say, it is impossible to cure mental disease from without, since it is a form of self-expression. We have to reach the It, that which lies behind all our activity, including our disease, and we have to influence it to see the world differently, to want to live. To administer drugs to a malfunctioning organism is to use blotting paper to mop up a spring of ink.

PNP bases itself on being as well as on becoming, on spontaneous flow between persons rather than on the false constructs of scientists. It lies between the glacier of isolation and the sea of social disappearance. It recognizes the need for and the possibility of a new kind of man who will ultimately find a way for human beings to live together without feeling it necessary to destroy themselves or others. It stands for growth and self-discovery in the company of others, seeing that the growth of oneself and others are inter-dependent.

By PNP I mean not only the network I have written about, but all movements and all efforts by men to help one another towards the ultimate goal. PNP is for Zen, for Zen is for people, and it is for *satori*, because *satori* is man finding himself. The Human Potential movement is PNP because there is no attempt in it to force upon individuals the ways of the world as decreed by those in power. It begins at the beginning, with people, and culminates there too. PNP expresses an idea. That idea is a potential reality.

PNP, the network PNP, is a beginning of a beginning. There have always been beginnings, some of them still-born, some of them to soon die, some to grow into world movements. PNP reflects a movement amongst men and women towards autonomy. It speaks of a rejection of authority based on social power or status. It rejects too the idea that we have to be taught how to live as ourselves, by experts. And it rejects the false ways of society, ways that do not match what is authentic in man. And in particular it repudiates the naïve attempts of men lost in unreal research on rats and the like to cure human beings of their ills in ways that simply lead them further away from themselves towards a state of partial stupor in which they will remain contrite and controlled. PNP says, somewhere deep inside it, we are all perfect, if we could but let it be. PNP is for you and me. For People, Not Psychiatry.

Postscript

Those who formed, fashioned, built and spread PNP, where are they now? Tarek is back in Egypt. Alma has set up house with Hugh, the man she went to Bali to meet, and is a mother. She lives in Ireland where Hugh is a professor. Bill Young got married and went to Canada to find the open land and skies and the good air he had always longed for. The Neilsons, Dave, Cathy, and Christopher Robin, are living peacefully and sweetly in Wales. Frank McAllan has left his job and plans to settle there too. David Eddy is teaching a bit and churning out novels one after the other. Jane Eddy soldiers on, mothering Charlotte and working in the system. Mike Williamson and John O'Shea finally left home and went to India, hated it and returned within a month. After a while as guests of Pam they moved out, and are coasting somewhere in London. Pete and Val Dunmow, after their year's stint at the helm of PNP (like a top sprinter, or an American pro footballer, you only have one or two good years at the heart of PNP), are working now on their own growth. Peter Wells is in Manchester, taking a diploma at the University. Others, like Neil Ormonde, Chris Cade, Graham Spowatt, I know nothing about. Jerry Rothenberg is in Primal therapy. He lives still at PNP house. Jenny James lives on there too, with Becky, nine now and growing lovely and fine. Jenny is running intensive groups with a neo-Reichian orientation. More importantly she is engrossed in her work and seems to have come to an acceptance of others that few equal. PNP house, once the rogue and scapegoat of the neighbourhood, is now in use by the locals as a haven of emotional release. Housewives come there to cry. Jack Lewis, Generous Jack, after doing a year's social work among the youths of Devon, is now giving neo-Reichian therapy in London. Pamela, my wife, lives close by

216

me, ploughing on with her Diploma of Education, finely and lovingly rearing our son Shem. As for Shem, nearly six now, he glides freely and easily between us, learning and teaching, a beautiful sturdy living being.

Addendum

All opinions are transient and dubious. This book is full of them. Some of them I no longer hold, may even laugh at. Never mind. We all have our ways to tread and none of them is free of error and foolishness. Besides, as far as opinion goes, and that world, I am already another.

Bibliography

This bibliography includes all books and articles mentioned in the text, plus other seminal and relevant publications.

Alexander, F. M., *The Resurrection of the Body*, Delta Books, 1969.

Assagioli, R., *Psychosynthesis*, The Viking Press, 1971.

Barnes, M. and Berke, J., *Two Accounts of A Journey Through Madness*, McGibbon & Kee, 1971.

Barnett, M., 'People Not Psychiatry', *New Society*, 31 December 1970.

Beckett, S., *Watt*, The Olympia Press, 1958.

Beckett, S., *Three Dialogues*, Calder & Boyars, 1965.

Beckett, S., *No's Knife*, Calder & Boyars, 1967.

Beckett, S., *End Game*, Faber & Faber, 1963.

Beckett, S., *Krapp's Last Tape*, Faber & Faber, 1959.

Berger, P. L., *Invitation to Sociology*, Pelican, 1966.

Berger, P. L. and Luckmann, T., *Social Construction of Reality*, Allen Lane, 1967.

Boadella, D., *Wilhelm Reich, The Evolution of His Work*, Vision Press, 1973.

Brown, N. O., *Life Against Death*, Routledge & Kegan Paul, 1959.

Brown, N. O., *Love's Body*, Vintage Books, 1966.

Buber, M., *The Knowledge of Man*, Allen & Unwin, 1965.

Butler, S., *The Way of all Flesh*, Penguin, 1966.

Castaneda, C., *The Teachings of Don Juan*, Penguin, 1970.

Castaneda, C., *A Separate Reality*, Bodley Head, 1971.

Castaneda, C. *A Journey to Ixtlan*, Bodley Head, 1973.

Christou, D., *The Logos of the Soul*, Dunquin Press, Vienna, 1963.

Coe, R. N., *Ionesco*, Oliver & Boyd, 1961.

Coomaraswamy, A. K., *Hinduism and Buddhism*, Philosophical Library, New York.

Cooper, D., *Psychiatry and Anti-Psychiatry*, Tavistock, 1967.

Cooper, D., *Death of the Family,* Allen Lane, 1971; Pelican, 1972.

Cooper, D. (ed.), *The Dialectics of Liberation*, Penguin, 1968.

Durkheim, K., *Hara*, Allen & Unwin, 1962.

Durrell, L., *Clea*, Faber & Faber, 1960.

Eliot, T. S., *Four Quartets*, Faber & Faber, 1944.

'Energy and Character', *The Journal of Bioenergetic Research*, Abbotsbury Publications, continuing.

Esterson, A., *The Leaves of Spring*, Tavistock, 1970.

Fagan, J. and Shepherd, I. L., *Gestalt Therapy Now*, Penguin, 1972.

Farquharson, R., *Drop Out!* Anthony Blond, 1968.

Foucault, M., *Madness and Civilization*, Tavistock, 1967.

Fowles, J., *The French Lieutenant's Woman*, Jonathan Cape, 1969.

Freud, S., *New Introductory Lectures*, The Hogarth Press, 1967.

Freud, S., *Delusion and Dream and Other Essays*, Beacon Press, 1956.

Genet, J., *The Balcony*, Faber & Faber, 1965.

Goffman, E., *Asylums*, Anchor Books, 1961.

Goffman, E., *Encounters*, Bobbs Merrill, 1961.

Goffman, E., *Stigma*, Penguin, 1968.

Goldmann, L., *The Human Sciences and Philosophy*, Jonathan Cape, 1969.

Gorz, A., *The Traitor*, Calder & Boyars, 1960.

Govinda, L. A., *Foundations of Tibetan Mysticism*, Rider, 1960.

Groddeck, G., *Exploring the Unconscious*, Vision Press, 1949.

Groddeck, G., *The Book of the It*, Vision Press, 1969.

Gurdjieff, G., *All and Everything*, Routledge & Kegan Paul, 1971.

Gurdjieff, G., *Meetings with Remarkable Men*, Routledge & Kegan Paul, 1963.

Hartmann, T. de, *Our Life with Mr Gurdjieff*, Penguin, 1972.

Hays, P., *New Horizons in Psychiatry*, Penguin, 1964.

Bibliography

Herrigel, E., *Zen in the Art of Archery*, Routledge & Kegan Paul, 1953.

Ionesco, E., *Rhinoceros*, Calder & Boyars, 1960.

Jackin, Harvey, *The Human Side of Human Beings*, Rational Island Publishers, Seattle.

Janov, A., *The Primal Scream*, Dell Publishing Co., 1970.

Janov, A., *The Anatomy of Mental Illness*, Putnam's 1971.

Kaufmann, W. *Nietzsche*, Meridian Books, 1956.

Kent, C., *The Puzzled Body*, Vision, 1970.

Kesey, K., *One Flew Over the Cuckoo's Nest*, Viking Press, 1970.

Kierkegaard, S., *The Sickness Unto Death*, Anchor Books, 1954.

Krishnamurti, J., *The Flight of the Eagle*, Servire Publishers, Wassenaar, 1971.

Laing, R. D., *The Divided Self*, Tavistock, 1960; Penguin, 1970.

Laing, R. D., *The Self and Others*, Tavistock, 1961.

Laing, R. D., *The Politics of Experience*, Penguin, 1967.

Laing, R. D., *Knots*, Tavistock, 1970; Penguin, 1972.

Laing, R. D. and Esterson, A., *Sanity, Madness and The Family*, Tavistock, 1964.

Leonard, G., *Education and Ecstasy*, J. Murray, 1970.

Lewis, H. R. and Streitfield, H. S., *Growth Games*, Bantam, 1972.

Lowen, A., *The Betrayal of the Body*, Collier-Macmillan, 1967.

Lowen, A., *Love and Orgasm*, Signet Books, New American Library.

Lutyens, M. (ed.), *The Penguin Krishnamurti Reader*, Penguin, 1970.

Marcuse, H., *Reason and Revolution*, Oxford University Press, 1941.

Marcuse, H., *Eros and Civilization*, Sphere Books, 1969.

Marcuse, H., *One-Dimensional Man*, Routledge & Kegan Paul, 1964; Sphere, 1968.

Marcuse, H., *Negations*, Allen Lane, 1968.

Maslow, A., *Towards a Psychology of Being*, Van Nostrand, Reinhold, 1962.

Miller, S., *Hot Springs*, Viking Press, 1971.

Milner, M. (as Joanna Field), *A Life of One's Own*, Allen & Unwin, 1965.

220

Milner, M., *On Not Being Able To Paint*, Heinemann, 1950.

Nietzsche, F., *Thus Spake Zarathustra*, Allen & Unwin, 1968.

Nietzsche, F., *The Gay Science*, Academic Press, 1866.

Nijinsky, V., *Diary*, Jonathan Cape, 1961.

Nuttall, J., *Bomb Culture*, MacGibbon & Kee, 1968.

Ouspensky, P., *The Fourth Way*, Routledge & Kegan Paul, 1957.

Ouspensky, P., *In Search of the Miraculous*, Routledge & Kegan Paul, 1950.

Parsons, T., *Social Structure and Personality*, The Free Press, 1964.

Perls, F. S., *Ego, Hunger and Aggression*, Vintage Books, 1969.

Perls, F. S., *Gestalt Therapy Verbatim*, Bantam Books, 1969.

Perls, F. S., *In and Out the Garbage Pail*, Real People Press, 1969.

Perls, F. S., Hefferline, R. and Goodman, P., *Gestalt Therapy*, Dell, 1951. Penguin, 1973.

Pesso, A., *Movement in Psychotherapy*, University of London Press, 1969.

Prather, H., *Notes to Myself*, Real People Press, 1970.

Reich, Wilhelm, *all works*.

Rilke, R. M., *Duino Elegies*, The Hogarth Press, 1939.

Rogers, C. R., *On Becoming a Person*, Constable, 1961.

Rogers, C. R., *Carl Rogers on Encounter Groups*, Harper & Row, 1970.

Rogers, C. R. and Dymond, R., *Psychotherapy and Personality Change*, University of Chicago Press, 1954.

Rogers, C. R. and Stevens, B., *Person to Person*, Real People Press, 1967.

Rosen, J. N., *Direct Analysis*, Grune & Stratton, 1953.

Sartre, J-P., *Being and Nothingness*, Methuen, 1969.

Sartre, J-P., *Saint Genet*, W. H. Allen, 1964.

Sartre, J-P., *Nausea*, Penguin, 1965.

Sartre, J-P., *Words*, Hamish Hamilton, 1964.

Schutz, W. C., *Joy*, Grove Press, 1967. Penguin, 1973.

Schutz, W. C., *Here Comes Everybody*, Harper & Row, 1971.

Stafford-Clark, D., *Psychiatry Today*, Pelican, 1963.

Stevens, B., *Don't Push the River*, Real People Press, 1970.

Bibliography

Szasz, T. S., *The Myth of Mental Illness*, Secker & Warburg, 1961.

Szasz, T. S., *The Ethics of Psychotherapy*, Delta Books, 1965.

Szasz, T. S., *The Manufacture of Madness*, Routledge & Kegan Paul, 1971.

Watts, A. W., *This Is It*, John Murray, 1961.

Watts, A. W., *The Way of Zen*, Pelican, 1962.

Watts, A. W., *Psychotherapy East and West*, Jonathan Cape, 1971.

Whyte, L. L., *The Next Development in Man*, Crescent, 1944; Tavistock, 1972.

Wilson, C., *The Outsider*, Victor Gollancz, 1956.

Wilson C., *The New Existentialism*.

Winnicott, D. W., *Collected Papers*, Tavistock, 1968.

Wittgenstein, L., *Tractatus Logico-Philosophicus*, Routledge & Kegan Paul, 1962.

Zorza, R., *The Right to Say 'We'*, Pall Mall, 1970.

Index

Index